NETWORK

The Right People... In the Right Places... For the Right Reasons

PARTICIPANT'S GUIDE

This Guide Belongs to:

_____

Bruce Bugbee · Don Cousins · Bill Hybels

ZondervanPublishingHouse
Grand Rapids, Michigan

A Division of HarperCollins*Publishers*

WILLOW CREEK RESOURCES

TO
VALERIE

For the many years

she has so faithfully

served me and our four children:

Brittany, Brianne, Bronwyn, and Todd.

Network: Participant's Guide
Copyright © 1994 by Willow Creek Community Church

Requests for information should be addressed to:
Zondervan Publishing House Grand Rapids, Michigan 49530

Edited by Jack Kuhatschek and Rachel Boers
Cover design by John M. Lucas
Interior design by Paetzold Design

ISBN 0-310-41231-5

All Scripture quotations, unless otherwise noted, are taken from *The Holy Bible: New International Version* ®. Copyright © 1973, 1978, 1984, by the International Bible Society. Used by permission of Zondervan Publishing House. All rights reserved.

Scripture quotations marked NASB are from the *New American Standard Bible*, copyright © 1960, 1962, 1963, 1968, 1971, 1972, 1973, 1975, 1977 by The Lockman Foundation.

98 99 00 01 02 03 04 /DC/ 28 27 26 25 24

CONTENTS

Willow Creek Resources® is a publishing partnership between Zondervan Publishing House and the Willow Creek Association®. Willow Creek Resources® includes drama sketches, small group curricula, training material, videos, and many other specialized ministry resources.

Willow Creek Association® is an international network of churches ministering to the unchurched. Founded in 1992, the Willow Creek Association® serves churches through conferences, seminars, regional roundtables, consulting, and ministry resource materials. The mission of the Association is to assist churches in reestablishing the priority and practice of reaching lost people for Christ through church ministries targeted to seekers.

For conference and seminar information please write to:

Willow Creek Association
P. O. Box 3188
Barrington, Illinois 60011-3188

FOREWORD

I consider the development of the Network materials to be one of the most significant breakthroughs in the history of Willow Creek Community Church.

We discovered years ago that believers flourish in their service to Christ when they are serving in the area of their giftedness and in conjunction with their God-given uniqueness. The Network materials grew out of our desire to help believers discover their spiritual gifts, and then determine where to use them in our church body.

The results of Network have been astounding. Imagine having fresh servants entering the work force of the church every year, confident of their giftedness and eager to invest them in service for God's glory.

It is happening!

May God bless you as you learn and grow through these tremendous materials.

Bill Hybels
Senior Pastor
Willow Creek Community Church

ACKNOWLEDGMENTS

It has been said that "there is nothing new under the sun" (Ecclesiastes 1:9). These Network materials bear witness to that timeless truth.

I have attempted to put together a simple and easy-to-walk-through process for believers who desire to serve in the local church. In doing so I have utilized the insights of many authors, teachers, leaders, and servants. This material has been adapted, edited, and written to present a comprehensive and consistent approach for those who desire to do ministry. But it could not have been done without the input and assistance of many people.

Peter Wagner's vision inspired me to see Spiritual Gifts understood, discovered, and used in ministry. His excellent seminar materials laid a foundation for my thinking.

Bill Hybels' teaching marked my understanding of Servant-hood and Servility. His insights are woven throughout these materials. He has provided leadership in the application of gift-based ministries.

Don Cousins contributed his understanding of ministries for greater clarity and practicality. His gifts of discernment and leadership have provided me a model of ministry that motivates me toward greater excellence in service.

Bobby Clinton provided awareness of several approaches for determining Spiritual Gifts in the book *Spiritual Gifts*.

The elders of Willow Creek Community Church faithfully exercised their oversight in the revision of these materials.

Lynne Hybels, Barb Engstrom, Juli Fillipini, and Jean Blount labored with love on the early manuscript and its many revisions.

Wendy Guthrie has made comprehensive contributions to the interactive learning that is now a part of Network. Her commitment to quality communication and biblical truth will benefit each participant. She has been a gracious project manager in the development of this new format.

John Nixdorf brought training expertise and perspective to the rewriting process. His patient and persistent spirit made an otherwise tedious task fun and meaningful.

Jim Mellado served as the catalyst to move the existing materials into this new international phase. He had started a Network Ministry and shares the passion and vision for what God is doing through the Network process.

I appreciate the Willow Creek Association℠ for its support and assistance in making these materials available to even greater numbers of believers. Their conferences have provided many exciting opportunities to present Network to Christian leaders around the world.

I want to thank the Fuller Institute of Evangelism and Church Growth for their distribution of the previous versions of Network. We share a common purpose.

And a special thanks to those who have participated in Network at Willow Creek Community Church. Your feedback and support have freed me to be more faithful and diligent in my own service to the body of Christ.

To all these people, and the many others who are so faithfully using their gifts, thank you. Together, we can serve yet a greater body of believers who want their lives to count for Christ and impact the world for which he died.

Bruce Bugbee
President
Network Ministries International

What's Network?

KEY SCRIPTURE VERSE: GALATIANS 5:13

O V E R V I E W

In this session you will:

1. Identify Network's Goal

2. Identify Network's Process

3. List two reasons for why we are to serve

4. Describe how we are to serve: *Servant Profile*

HUDDLE GROUP: IMAGINE A CHURCH

DIRECTIONS

1. Introduce yourself to your group.

2. Tell why you've come to Network.

3. Discuss what observations and insights you had from the video, and why.

INTRODUCTION TO NETWORK

NETWORK'S GOAL

Network's Goal is to help believers to be

_____ *Fruitful* _____ and

_____ *fulfilled* _____ in a

meaningful place of service.

You, my brothers, were called to be free. But do not use your freedom to indulge the sinful nature; rather, **serve one another in love.** (Gal. 5:13)

INTRODUCTION TO NETWORK

Motion Without Movement

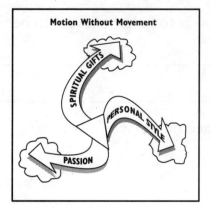

Making A Mark

INTRODUCTION TO NETWORK

Like a Pile of Puzzle Pieces

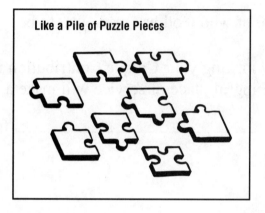

Like a Pile of Puzzle Pieces

Network Puts the Pieces Together

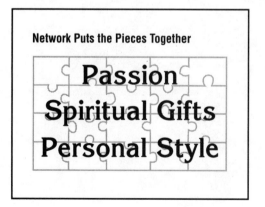

Network Puts the Pieces Together

Passion
Spiritual Gifts
Personal Style

INTRODUCTION TO NETWORK

Network will help you understand:

More of who God has made you to be.

How making your Unique Contribution in a meaningful place of service will make a

kingdom difference for eternity.

INTRODUCTION TO NETWORK

NETWORK'S PROCESS

Step One: _DISCOVERY   (class)_

You learn more about your God-given

_____shape_____.

Step Two: _Consultation_____

A consultant assists you in finding a meaningful place of service, your ministry

_____Fit_____.

Step Three: _Service_____

The_____Goal_____ is service.

STEP ONE: DISCOVERY

WHY WE ARE TO SERVE

The purpose for serving in the church is to

- _glorify God_
- _edify others_

We see this in many places in scripture, but there are two key passages:

1. The Ten Commandments (Ex. 20:1–17)

The first four commandments describe how we are to

love God.

The remaining six commandments describe how we

are to _love others_.

2. The Great Commandment

Love the Lord your God with all your heart and with all your soul and with all your mind. This is the first and greatest commandment. And the second is like it: Love your neighbor as yourself. All the Law and the Prophets hang on these two commandments. (Matt. 22:37–40)

STEP ONE: DISCOVERY

How Does Serving Glorify God?

Service is a ___worship___ and worship glorifies God.

Whoever speaks, let him speak, as it were, the utter-
ances of God; whoever serves, let him do so as by
the strength which God supplies; so that in all things
God may be glorified through Jesus Christ, to whom
belongs the glory and dominion forever and ever,
Amen. (1 Peter 4:11 NASB)

How Does Serving Edify Others?

Serving ___builds up___

(edifies) the church.

It was he who gave some to be apostles, some to
be prophets, some to be evangelists, and some to be
pastors and teachers, to prepare God's people for
works of service, **so *that the body of Christ may be***
built up. (Eph. 4:11-12)

Glorifying God and edifying each other is the
major test of service!

9

STEP ONE: DISCOVERY

HOW WE ARE TO SERVE

Servant Profile

Passion

Your Passion indicates ___where___
you are best suited to serve.

There is no right or wrong Passion.

Spiritual Gifts

Spiritual Gifts indicate ___what___
you will do when you serve.

There are no right or wrong Spiritual Gifts

Personal Style

Personal Style indicates ___how___
you will serve.

There is no right or wrong Personal Style.

SESSION 1 SUMMARY

Network's Goal:

- Helping you to be fruitful and fulfilled in a meaningful place of service

Network's Process that will help us reach that goal:

- Discovery

- Consultation

- Service

Why we are to serve:

- Glorify God

- Edify others

How we are to serve, according to our *Servant Profile:*

- Passion

- Spiritual Gifts

- Personal Style

Where Should I Serve?

KEY SCRIPTURE PASSAGE: PSALM 37:3–5

O V E R V I E W

In this session you will:

1. Define Passion and list its three key characteristics

2. Complete the *Passion Assessment*

3. Identify one or more possible Passion areas

4. Gain a clearer understanding of your Passion

PASSION

CHARACTERISTICS

Passion is ___God given desire___.

There is no right or wrong Passion.

Passion answers the "___where___" question.

DEFINITION

Passion is the God-given desire that compels us to make a difference in a particular ministry.

dream

Trust in the LORD, and do good; Dwell in the land and cultivate faithfulness. Delight yourself in the LORD; And He will give you the desires of your heart. Commit your way to the LORD, Trust also in Him, and He will do it. (Ps. 37:3-5 NASB)

But when God, who set me apart from birth and called me by his grace, was pleased to reveal his Son in me so that I might preach him among the Gentiles, I did not consult any man . . . (Gal. 1:15-16)

PASSION ASSESSMENT

An important part of discovering your *Servant Profile* is understanding your Passion. When you have a Passion for an area of ministry, you are more enthusiastic and motivated to serve.

DIRECTIONS

1. Prayerfully consider your answers to the questions.
2. Complete the assessment on your own.
3. There are no right or wrong responses.
4. Don't be concerned about "whether" you can do it or "how" it can be done.
5. Complete the assessment as if you have no obstacles to fulfilling your heart's desire.

QUESTIONS

1. If I could snap my fingers and know that I couldn't fail, what would I do?

    Feed the hungry

2. At the end of my life, I'd love to be able to look back and know that I'd done something about:

    hunger

3. If I were to mention your name to a group of your friends, what would they say you were really interested in or passionate about?

    med tech, tennis, photography, music, social concerns

PASSION ASSESSMENT

4. What conversation would keep you talking late into the night?

_____

_____

_____

At this point, if you are able to describe your Passion in a word or brief sentence, go to Item 10 of this assessment and do so. If you would like more clarification, consider the following statements.

5. What I would most like to do for others is:

_____

_____

_____

6. The people I would like to help most are:

❑ Infants	❑ Children	❑ Youth
❑ Teen moms	❑ Single parents	❑ College students
❑ Divorced	❑ Widowed	❑ Singles
❑ Career women	❑ Young marrieds	❑ Refugees
❑ Parents	❑ Empty nesters	❑ Homeless
❑ Unemployed	☑ Elderly	❑ Disabled
❑ Prisoners	❑ Poor	❑ Hospitalized

❑ Others: _____

PASSION ASSESSMENT

7. The issues or causes I feel strongly about are:

❑ Environment	❑ Child care	❑ Homosexuality
❑ Discipleship	❑ AIDS	❑ Politics
❑ Violence	☒ Injustice	❑ Racism
❑ Education	❑ Addictions	❑ International
❑ Economic	❑ Reaching the lost	❑ Technology
❑ Health care	❑ Poverty	❑ Family
❑ Abortion	☒ Hunger	❑ Literacy
❑ Church		

❑ Others: _____

8. The following exercise may help you uncover a theme from your experience which will give you insight into your Passion.

List the top five to seven positive experiences you've had in your life and briefly describe what you did and why it was meaningful to you.

These experiences may have taken place at home, work, school, or during your free time. It may have been a clock you fixed or a dress you made. It may have been a puzzle you put together or an award you received. It may have been helping some friends move, building a house, winning an election, or giving to someone in need. Remember, these are experiences that you enjoyed doing and felt fulfilled.

PASSION ASSESSMENT

Five to Seven Positive Experiences	Why This Experience Is Meaningful To Me
a. Ch + Soc newsltr	kept myself + others informed
b. acing college exams	
c. chairing state conv.	challenge
d. teaching appreciative students	expertise recognized (CPA, RN in service)
e.	
f.	
g.	

Next, read through what you have written and look for an underlying theme. If one or two come to mind, write them in the space below.

_____

_____

_____

PASSION ASSESSMENT

SUMMARY

9. I think the area where I could make the most

significant contribution is: ————————————————————

————————————————————————————————————

If you need more help in identifying your Passion, look for patterns
in your answers. For example, can you see any themes? Does a
particular age group keep coming up? Is there a need that keeps
surfacing? Are you serving in a similar role in different areas?
Can you prioritize your concerns?

CONCLUSION

10. Based on my answers to the above questions, I sense *I have a*

Passion for: ————————————————————————————

———— hunger   music   teaching ————————

Making a statement of Passion is not easy for everyone. Remember
that this is just the beginning of the process of identifying and
clarifying your Passion. As you think, pray, and gain more ministry
experience, your Passion will become more clear over time.

PASSION CLARIFICATION

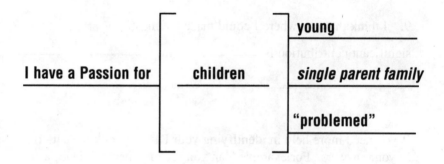

TED

I have a Passion for | children | young

single parent family

"problemed"

SUE

I have a Passion for | reaching the lost | all

family & friends

neighborhood

coworkers

children

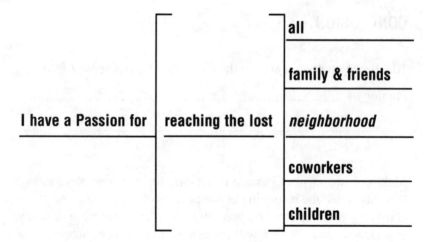

HUDDLE GROUP: CLARIFY YOUR PASSION

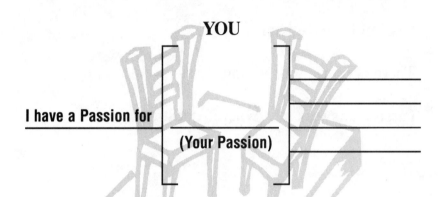

YOU

I have a Passion for

(Your Passion)

DIRECTIONS

1. Each explain your Passion.

2. Discuss each person's Passion to help that person gain a clearer understanding of his or her Passion.

3. Use the worksheet above to note key words or phrases that clarify your Passion.

WRAP-UP

1. Look at the ideas you came up with in your huddle group.

2. Circle the idea that best reflects your Passion, then transfer your Passion to your *Servant Profile* on p.124 in your Participant's Guide.

SESSION 2 SUMMARY

Passion is God-given.

There is no right or wrong Passion.

Passion answers the "where" question.

Why Can't You Be More Like Me?

KEY SCRIPTURE PASSAGE: 1 CORINTHIANS 12

In this session you will:

1. Define Spiritual Gifts, and list their three key characteristics

2. List the three elements of serving as a body in the church

3. Describe one step to take to become more interdependent

4. Identify two key points concerning diversity

WHAT IS A SPIRITUAL GIFT?

CHARACTERISTICS

Spiritual Gifts are ___God-given___.

There are no right or wrong Spiritual Gifts.

Spiritual Gifts answer the "___WHAT___" question.

WHAT IS A SPIRITUAL GIFT?

SPIRITUAL GIFT DEFINITION

Spiritual Gifts Are _Special Abilities_

- Spiritual Gifts are divine endowments
- They are abilities God has given to us to make our Unique Contribution

(1 Cor. 12:7)

Distributed By The _Holy Spirit_

- Spiritual Gifts are given by God
- He bestows Spiritual Gifts to us for meaningful service

(1 Cor. 12:11)

To Every _Believer_ **According To**

God's _Design_ **And** _Grace_

- Every believer has at least one Spiritual Gift
- Every believer is a minister

(1 Peter 4:10)

For The _Common Good_ **Of The Body Of Christ**

- The Spiritual Gifts that God gives us allow us to serve one another better
- A major test of our use of Spiritual Gifts is to glorify God and edify others

(1 Cor. 12:7)

25

UNIQUENESS OF THE BELIEVER

God has carefully selected each believer's Spiritual Gift and place of service within the body.

Our *Servant Profiles* are not of our choosing, they are by God's design.

> Now to **each one** the manifestation of the Spirit is given for the common good. (1 Cor. 12:7)

> All these are the work of one and the same Spirit, and he **gives them to each one, just as he determines.** (1 Cor. 12:11)

> But in fact God has arranged the parts in the body, every one of them, **just as he wanted** them to be. (1 Cor. 12:18)

We have each been given a ___UNIQUE___ role to play.

DIVERSITY OF BELIEVERS

Each of us has a unique design.

There is great diversity in the body.

Our differences are by God's design.

> *To one there is given through the Spirit the message of wisdom, to another the message of knowledge by means of the same Spirit, to another faith by the same Spirit, to another gifts of healing by that one Spirit, to another miraculous powers, to another prophecy, to another distinguishing between spirits, to another speaking in different kinds of tongues, and to still another the interpretation of tongues. (1 Cor. 12:8–10)*

INTERDEPENDENCE OF BELIEVERS

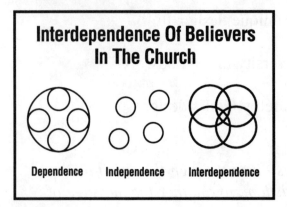

Interdependence Of Believers In The Church

Dependence   Independence   Interdependence

Dependence

Independence

Culturally we have equated ___MATURITY___
with independence.

Interdependence

God's design is that we serve like a body

> *...so in Christ we who are many form one body, and each member belongs to all the others.* (Rom. 12:5)

> *Now you are the body of Christ, and each one of you is a part of it.* (1 Cor. 12:27)

INTERDEPENDENCE OF BELIEVERS

HUDDLE GROUP: INTERDEPENDENCE

Directions
1. Share with your group what keeps you, personally, from being more interdependent.

2. Identify one step you could take to become more interdependent.

3. Write your answers in the space provided.

What keeps me from being more interdependent?

lack of trust, pride, loss of control, lack of efficiency, fear of conflict, failure

---

One step I could take to become more interdependent:

relax + trust

DIVERSITY IS NOT DIVISION

As it is, there are many parts, but one body. The eye cannot say to the hand, "I don't need you!"

...so that there should be no division in the body, but that its parts should have equal concern for each other. If one part suffers, every part suffers with it; if one part is honored, every part rejoices with it. (1 Cor. 12:20–21a, 25–26)

want best for others, Claudia

We are all diverse, but we are called to serve without division.

1 Corinthians 12:4-6

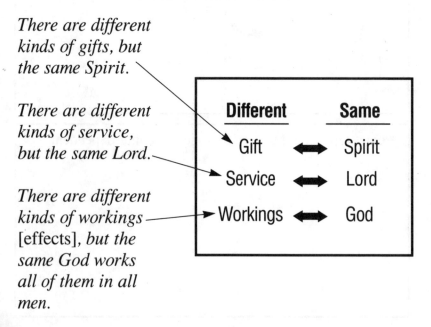

There are different kinds of gifts, but the same Spirit.

There are different kinds of service, but the same Lord.

There are different kinds of workings [effects], *but the same God works all of them in all men.*

Different		Same
Gift ⟷		Spirit
Service ⟷		Lord
Workings ⟷		God

UNITY IS NOT CONFORMITY

If the whole body were an eye, where would the sense of hearing be? If the whole body were an ear, where would the sense of smell be? But in fact God has arranged the parts in the body, every one of them, just as he wanted them to be. If they were all one part, where would the body be? As it is, there are many parts, but one body.
(1 Cor. 12:17–20)

Are all apostles? Are all prophets? Are all teachers? Do all work miracles? Do all have gifts of healing? Do all speak in tongues? Do all interpret? (1 Cor. 12:29–30)

Unity is not achieved by being alike.

Unity is achieved by having the _Same   purpose_: to glorify God and edify others.

SESSION 3 SUMMARY

DEFINITION:

Spiritual Gifts are special abilities distributed by the Holy Spirit to every believer according to God's design and grace for the common good of the body of Christ.

CHARACTERISTICS:

• Spiritual Gifts are God-given.

• There are no right or wrong Spiritual Gifts.

• Spiritual Gifts answer the "what" question.

God has designed each part of the body to be in an interdependent relationship with all the other parts.

What Am I Supposed to Do?

KEY SCRIPTURE PASSAGE: ROMANS 12:6–8

In this session you will:

1. List the Spiritual Gifts from the Bible passages provided

2 Match each Spiritual Gift with its corresponding characteristic

3. Identify Spiritual Gifts in action

4. Identify how Spiritual Gifts are affirmed

GROUP EXERCISE: SPIRITUAL GIFTS MENTIONED IN SCRIPTURE

DIRECTIONS

1. As each scripture passage is read, and each Spiritual Gift is identified, write that Spiritual Gift in the space provided in your Participant's Guide.

2. A few of the Spiritual Gifts occur more than once, but you only need to write a Spiritual Gift down the first time it occurs.

Scripture Passage	Gifts Mentioned
1 CORINTHIANS 12:8–10 *For to one is given the word of wisdom through the Spirit, and to another the word of knowledge according to the same Spirit; to another faith by the same spirit, and to another gifts of healing by the one Spirit, and to another the effecting of miracles, and to another prophecy, and to another the distinguishing of spirits, to another various kinds of tongues, and to another the interpretation of tongues.* NASB	1. wisdom 2. knowledge 3. faith 4. healing 5. miracles 6. prophecy 7. discernment 8. tongues 9. interpretation
1 CORINTHIANS 12:28 *And God has appointed in the church, first apostles, second prophets, third teachers, then miracles, the gifts of healings, helps, administrations, various kinds of tongues.* NASB	10. apostleship 11. teaching 12. helps 13. administration

GROUP EXERCISE: SPIRITUAL GIFTS MENTIONED IN SCRIPTURE

ROMANS 12:6–8 *And since we have gifts that differ according to the grace given to us, let each exercise them accordingly: if prophecy, according to the proportion of his faith; if service,* (helps) *in his serving; or he who teaches, in his teaching; or he who exhorts, in his exhortation; he who gives, with liberality; he who leads, with diligence; he who shows mercy, with cheerfulness.* NASB	14. *encouragement* 15. *giving* 16. *leadership* 17. *mercy*
EPHESIANS 4:11 *And He gave some as apostles, and some as prophets, and some as evangelists, and some as pastors and teachers.* NASB	18. *evangelism* 19. *shepherding*

NOTE: The lists of Spiritual Gifts provided in the Bible are not identical, but they vary in order and content. The biblical lists shown in Network are illustrative rather than exhaustive.

1 PETER 4:9–10 *Be hospitable to one another without complaint. As each one has received a special gift, employ it in serving one another, as good stewards of the manifold grace of God.* NASB	20. *hospitality*

GROUP EXERCISE: SPIRITUAL GIFTS MENTIONED IN SCRIPTURE

EXODUS 31:3 *And I have filled him with the Spirit of God in wisdom, in understanding, in knowledge, and in all kinds of craftsmanship.* NASB	21. *Craftsmanship*
1 TIMOTHY 2:1–2 *I urge, then, first of all, that requests, prayers, intercession and thanksgiving be made for everyone—for kings and all those in authority, that we may live peaceful and quiet lives in all godliness and holiness.*	22. *intercession*
PSALM 150:3–5 *Praise Him with trumpet sound; Praise Him with harp and lyre. Praise Him with timbrel and dancing; Praise Him with stringed instruments and pipe. Praise Him with loud cymbals; Praise Him with resounding cymbals.* NASB	23. *Arts* *Creative* *Communication*

NOTE: Some churches would affirm other possible Spiritual Gifts, not described or mentioned in Network. Some of those Spiritual Gifts might include, but are not necessarily limited to: celibacy, counseling, exorcism, martyrdom, and voluntary poverty.

HUDDLE GROUP: SPIRITUAL GIFTS MATCHING

DIRECTIONS

1. Read each characteristic aloud.

2. Match each characteristic with its corresponding Spiritual Gift.

3. Write the letter of the characteristic in the blank under "matches," which is in the Spiritual Gifts column.

4. The characteristic for each Spiritual Gift is found in the same group as the Spiritual Gift itself.

HUDDLE GROUP: SPIRITUAL GIFTS MATCHING

GROUP 1

Spiritual Gift	Contributes	Characteristic
1. Administration Matches: __B__	*efficiency*	A. The divine ability to start and oversee the development of new churches or ministry structures. People with this gift: pioneer and establish new ministries or churches; adapt to different surroundings by being culturally sensitive and aware; desire to minister to unreached people in other communities or countries; have responsibilities to oversee ministries or groups of churches; demonstrate authority and vision for the mission of the church.
2. Apostleship Matches: __A__	*new ministry*	B. The divine enablement to understand what makes an organization function, and the special ability to plan and execute procedures that accomplish the goals of the ministry. People with this gift: develop strategies or plans to reach identified goals; assist ministries to become more effective and efficient; create order out of organizational chaos; manage or coordinate a variety of responsibilities to accomplish a task; organize people, tasks, or events.
3. Craftsmanship Matches: __D__	*skill*	C. The divine enablement to distinguish between truth and error, to discern the spirits, differentiating between good and evil, right and wrong. People with this gift: distinguish truth from error, right from wrong, pure motives from impure; identify deception in others with accuracy and appropriateness; determine whether a word attributed to God is authentic; recognize inconsistencies in a teaching, prophetic message, or interpretation; are able to sense the presence of evil.

HUDDLE GROUP: SPIRITUAL GIFTS MATCHING

GROUP 1, cont.

Spiritual Gift	Contributes	Characteristic
4. Creative Communication **Matches:** F	*artistic expression*	D. The divine enablement to creatively design and/or construct items to be used for ministry. People with this gift: work with wood, cloth, paints, metal, glass, and other raw materials; make things which increase the effectiveness of others' ministries; enjoy serving with their hands to meet tangible needs; design and build tangible items and resources for ministry use; work with different kinds of tools and are skilled with their hands.
5. Discernment **Matches:** C	*clarity*	E. The divine enablement to present truth so as to strengthen, comfort, or urge to action those who are discouraged or wavering in their faith. People with this gift: come to the side of those who are discouraged to strengthen and reassure them; challenge, comfort, or confront others to trust and hope in the promises of God; urge others to action by applying biblical truth; motivate others to grow; emphasize God's promises and to have confidence in his will.
6. Encouragement **Matches:** E	*affirmation*	F. The divine enablement to communicate God's truth through a variety of art forms. People with this gift: use the arts to communicate God's truth; develop and use artistic skills such as drama, writing, art, music, dance, etc.; use variety and creativity to captivate people and cause them to consider Christ's message; challenge people's perspective of God through various forms of the arts; demonstrate fresh ways to express the Lord's ministry and message.

HUDDLE GROUP: SPIRITUAL GIFTS MATCHING

GROUP 2

Spiritual Gift	Contributes	Characteristic
7. Evangelism Matches: K	good news	G. The divine enablement to accomplish practical and necessary tasks which free-up, support, and meet the needs of others. People with this gift: serve behind the scenes wherever needed to support the gifts and ministries of others; see the tangible and practical things to be done and enjoy doing them; sense God's purpose and pleasure in meeting every day responsibilities; attach spiritual value to practical service; enjoy knowing that they are freeing up others to do what God has called them to do.
8. Faith Matches: I	confidence	H. The divine enablement to care for people by providing fellowship, food, and shelter. People with this gift: provide an environment where people feel valued and cared for; meet new people and help them to feel welcomed; create a safe and comfortable setting where relationships can develop; seek ways to connect people together into meaningful relationships; set people at ease in unfamiliar surroundings.
9. Giving Matches: J	resources	I. The divine enablement to act on God's promises with confidence and unwavering belief in God's ability to fulfill his purposes. People with this gift: believe the promises of God and inspire others to do the same; act in complete confidence of God's ability to overcome obstacles; demonstrate an attitude of trust in God's will and his promises; advance the cause of Christ because they go forward when others will not; ask God for what is needed and trust him for his provision.

HUDDLE GROUP: SPIRITUAL GIFTS MATCHING

GROUP 2, cont.

Spiritual Gift	Contributes	Characteristic
10. Healing **Matches:** ___L___	wholeness	J. The divine enablement to contribute money and resources to the work of the Lord with cheerfulness and liberality. People with this gift do not ask, "How much money do I need to give to God?" but "How much money do I need to live on?" People with this gift: manage their finances and limit their lifestyle in order to give as much of their resources as possible; support the work of ministry with sacrificial gifts to advance the Kingdom; meet tangible needs that enable spiritual growth to occur; provide resources, generously and cheerfully, trusting God for his provision; may have a special ability to make money so that they may use it to further God's work.
11. Helps (Serving) **Matches:** ___G___	support	K. The divine enablement to effectively communicate the gospel to unbelievers so they respond in faith and move toward discipleship. People with this gift: communicate the message of Christ with clarity and conviction; seek out opportunities to talk to unbelievers about spiritual matters; challenge unbelievers to faith and to become fully devoted followers of Christ; adapt their presentation of the gospel to connect with the individual's needs; seek opportunities to build relationships with unbelievers.
12. Hospitality **Matches:** ___H___	acceptance	L. The divine enablement to be God's means for restoring people to wholeness. People with this gift: demonstrate the power of God; bring restoration to the sick and diseased; authenticate a message from God through healing; use it as an opportunity to communicate a biblical truth and to see God glorified; pray, touch, or speak words that miraculously bring healing to one's body.

HUDDLE GROUP: SPIRITUAL GIFTS MATCHING

GROUP 3

Spiritual Gift	Contributes	Characteristic
13. Intercession Matches: ___N___	protection	M. The divine enablement to authenticate the ministry and message of God through supernatural interventions which glorify him. People with this gift: speak God's truth and have it authenticated by an accompanying miracle; express confidence in God's faithfulness and ability to manifest his presence; bring the ministry and message of Jesus Christ with power; claim God to be the source of the miracle and glorify him; represent Christ and through the gift point people to a relationship with Christ.
14. Interpretation Matches: ___R___	under-standing	N. The divine enablement to consistently pray on behalf of and for others, seeing frequent and specific results. People with this gift: feel compelled to earnestly pray on behalf of someone or some cause; have a daily awareness of the spiritual battles being waged and pray; are convinced God moves in direct response to prayer; pray in response to the leading of the spirit, whether they understand it or not; exercise authority and power for the protection of others and the equipping of them to serve.
15. Knowledge Matches: ___P___	awareness	O. The divine enablement to cast vision, motivate, and direct people to harmoniously accomplish the purposes of God. People with this gift: provide direction for God's people or ministry; motivate others to perform to the best of their abilities; present the "big picture" for others to see; model the values of the ministry; take responsibility and establish goals.

HUDDLE GROUP: SPIRITUAL GIFTS MATCHING

GROUP 3, cont.

Spiritual Gift	Contributes	Characteristic
16. Leadership **Matches:** _O_	direction	P. The divine enablement to bring truth to the body through a revelation or biblical insight. People with this gift: receive truth which enables them to better serve the body; search the scriptures for insight, understanding, and truth; gain knowledge which at times was not attained by natural means; have an unusual insight or understanding that serves the church; organize information for teaching and practical use.
17. Mercy **Matches:** _Q_	care	Q. The divine enablement to cheerfully and practically help those who are suffering or are in need, compassion moved to action. People with this gift: focus upon alleviating the sources of pain or discomfort in suffering people; address the needs of the lonely and forgotten; express love, grace, and dignity to those facing hardships and crisis; serve in difficult or unsightly circumstances and do so cheerfully; concern themselves with individual or social issues that oppress people.
18. Miracles **Matches:** _M_	power	R. The divine enablement to make known to the body of Christ the message of one who is speaking in tongues. People with this gift: respond to a message spoken in tongues by giving an interpretation; glorify God and demonstrate his power through this miraculous manifestation; edify the body by interpreting a timely message from God; understand an unlearned language and communicate that message to the body of Christ; are sometimes prophetic when exercising an interpretation of tongues for the church.

HUDDLE GROUP: SPIRITUAL GIFTS MATCHING

GROUP 4

Spiritual Gift	Contributes	Characteristic
19. Prophecy Matches: ___W___	*conviction*	S. The divine enablement to understand, clearly explain, and apply the word of God causing greater Christ likeness in the lives of listeners. People with this gift: communicate biblical truth that inspires greater obedience to the word; challenge listeners simply and practically with the truths of scripture; present the whole counsel of God for maximum life change; give attention to detail and accuracy; prepare through extended times of study and reflection.
20. Shepherding Matches: ___T___	*nurture*	T. The divine enablement to nurture, care for, and guide people toward on-going spiritual maturity and becoming like Christ. People with this gift: take responsibility to nurture the whole person in their walk with God; provide guidance and oversight to a group of God's people; model with their life what it means to be a fully devoted follower of Jesus; establish trust and confidence through long-term relationships; lead and protect those within their span of care.
21. Teaching Matches: ___S___	*application*	U. The divine enablement to speak, worship, or pray in a language unknown to the speaker. People with this gift may receive a spontaneous message from God which is made known to his body through the gift of Interpretation. People with this gift: express with an interpretation a word by the Spirit which edifies the body; communicate a message given by God for the church; speak in a language they have never learned and do not understand; worship the Lord with unknown words too deep for the mind to comprehend; experience an intimacy with God which inspires them to serve and edify others.

HUDDLE GROUP: SPIRITUAL GIFTS MATCHING

GROUP 4, cont.

Spiritual Gift	Contributes	Characteristic
22.Tongues **Matches:** _____U_____	message	V. The divine enablement to apply spiritual truth effectively to meet a need in a specific situation. People with this gift: focus on the unseen consequences in determining the next steps to take; receive an understanding of what is necessary to meet the needs of the body; provide divinely given solutions in the midst of conflict and confusion; hear the Spirit provide direction for God's best in a given situation; apply spiritual truth in specific and practical ways.
23.Wisdom **Matches:** _____✓_____	guidance	W. The divine enablement to reveal truth and proclaim it in a timely and relevant manner for understanding, correction, repentance or edification. There may be immediate or future implications. People with this gift: expose sin or deception in others for the purpose of reconciliation; speak a timely word from God causing conviction, repentance, and edification; see truth that others often fail to see and challenge them to respond; warn of God's immediate or future judgment if there is no repentance; under stand God's heart and mind through experiences he takes them through.

VIDEO VIGNETTE: SPIRITUAL GIFTS IN ACTION

DIRECTIONS

1. As you watch this video see if you can identify which Spiritual Gifts each character may have.

2. Write each Spiritual Gift you identify in the space provided:

_____

_____

_____

_____

_____

_____

_____

The true and final test of your Spiritual Gift is through the affirmation of the

_____ body of Christ _____ .

SPIRITUAL GIFT ASSESSMENT

DIRECTIONS

1. Respond to each statement on the *Spiritual Gift Assessment* pages which follow, according to the following scale:

   3 = Consistently, definitely true
   2 = Most of the time, usually true
   1 = Some of the time, once in a while
   0 = Not at all, never

2. Using response sheet below, write your response to each statement in the block whose number corresponds to that number statement in the *Spiritual Gift Assessment*.

3. **Important: Answer according to who you are, not who you would like to be or think you ought to be.** How true are these statements of you? What has been your experience? To what degree do these statements reflect your usual tendencies?

1	2	3	4	5	6	7	8	9	10	11	12	13	14	15	16	17	18	19
3	0	0	1	2	2	1	2	2	1	0	1	0	1	1	2	1	1	1
20	**21**	**22**	**23**	**24**	**25**	**26**	**27**	**28**	**29**	**30**	**31**	**32**	**33**	**34**	**35**	**36**	**37**	**38**
3	1	0	2	0	1	0	3	1	1	1	1	2	1	2	1	1	2	1
39	**40**	**41**	**42**	**43**	**44**	**45**	**46**	**47**	**48**	**49**	**50**	**51**	**52**	**53**	**54**	**55**	**56**	**57**
1	1	0	0	1	1	1	2	1	0	0	1	1	1	1	1	1	2	1
58	**59**	**60**	**61**	**62**	**63**	**64**	**65**	**66**	**67**	**68**	**69**	**70**	**71**	**72**	**73**	**74**	**75**	**76**
2	2	0	1	1	1	0	2	1	2	0	3	1	2	2	1	2	1	2
77	**78**	**79**	**80**	**81**	**82**	**83**	**84**	**85**	**86**	**87**	**88**	**89**	**90**	**91**	**92**	**93**	**94**	**95**
1	1	1	1	1	1	1	2	3	0	0	1	0	1	2	3	2	1	2
96	**97**	**98**	**99**	**100**	**101**	**102**	**103**	**104**	**105**	**106**	**107**	**108**	**109**	**110**	**111**	**112**	**113**	**114**
1	1	1	1	1	1	1	1	2	1	1	2	1	1	1	1	0	2	2
115	**116**	**117**	**118**	**119**	**120**	**121**	**122**	**123**	**124**	**125**	**126**	**127**	**128**	**129**	**130**	**131**	**132**	**133**
3	0	0	0	2	0	0	1	1	1	1	1	3	2	1	0	1	2	2
T O T A L																		
14	6	2	6	8	7	4	13	11	6	3	10	8	9	10	9	8	11	11
A	**B**	**C**	**D**	**E**	**F**	**G**	**H**	**I**	**J**	**K**	**L**	**M**	**N**	**O**	**P**	**Q**	**R**	**S**

SPIRITUAL GIFT ASSESSMENT

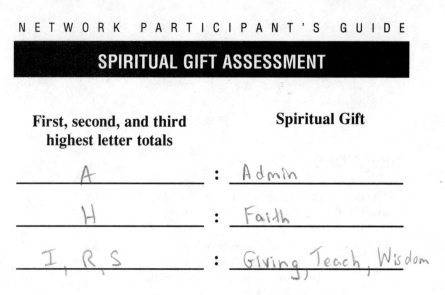

First, second, and third highest letter totals	Spiritual Gift
_A_	: _Admin_
_H_	: _Faith_
_I, R, S_	: _Giving, Teach, Wisdom_

Transfer these conclusions to p.71 of this guide.

SPIRITUAL GIFT ASSESSMENT KEY

A = Administration
B = Apostleship
C = Craftsmanship _– last_
D = Creative Communication
E = Discernment
F = Encouragement
G = Evangelism _– low_
H = Faith
I = Giving
J = Helps
K = Hospitality _– low_
L = Intercession
M = Knowledge
N = Leadership
O = Mercy
P = Prophecy
Q = Shepherding
R = Teaching
S = Wisdom

Healing, Interpretation, Miracles, and Tongues are not included in the *Spiritual Gift Assessment* or *Observation Assessment* because their presence in the life of a believer tends to be self-evident.

SPIRITUAL GIFT ASSESSMENT

1. I like to organize people, tasks, and events.

2. I would like to start churches in places where they do not presently exist.

3. I enjoy working creatively with wood, cloth, paints, metal, glass, or other materials.

4. I enjoy challenging people's perspective of God by using various forms of art.

5. I can readily distinguish between spiritual truth and error, good and evil.

6. I tend to see the potential in people.

7. I communicate the gospel to others with clarity and effectiveness.

8. I find it natural and easy to trust God to answer my prayers.

9. I give liberally and joyfully to people in financial need or to projects requiring support.

10. I enjoy working behind the scenes to support the work of others.

11. I view my home as a place to minister to people in need.

12. I take prayer requests from others and consistently pray for them.

13. I am approached by people who want to know my perspective on a particular passage or biblical truth.

14. I am able to motivate others to accomplish a goal.

15. I empathize with hurting people and desire to help in their healing process.

16. I can speak in a way that results in conviction and change in the lives of others.

17. I enjoy spending time nurturing and caring for others.
18. I am able to communicate God's word effectively.

19. I am often sought out by others for advice about spiritual or personal matters.

20. I am careful, thorough, and skilled at managing details.

SPIRITUAL GIFT ASSESSMENT

21. I am attracted to the idea of serving in another country or ethnic community.

22. I am skilled in working with different kinds of tools.

23. I enjoy developing and using my artistic skills (art, drama, music, photography, etc.).

24. I frequently am able to judge a person's character based upon first impressions.

25. I enjoy reassuring and strengthening those who are discouraged.

26. I consistently look for opportunities to build relationships with non-Christians.

27. I have confidence in God's continuing provision and help, even in difficult times.

28. I give more than a tithe so that kingdom work can be accomplished.

29. I enjoy doing routine tasks that support the ministry.

30. I enjoy meeting new people and helping them to feel welcomed.

31. I enjoy praying for long periods of time and receive leadings as to what God wants me to pray for.

32. I receive information from the Spirit that I did not acquire through natural means.

33. I am able to influence others to achieve a vision.

34. I can patiently support those going through painful experiences as they try to stabilize their lives.

35. I feel responsible to confront others with the truth.

36. I have compassion for wandering believers and want to protect them.

37. I can spend time in study knowing that presenting truth will make a difference in the lives of people.

38. I can often find simple, practical solutions in the midst of conflict or confusion.

SPIRITUAL GIFT ASSESSMENT

39. I can clarify goals and develop strategies or plans to accomplish them.

40. I am willing to take an active part in starting a new church.

41. I enjoy making things for use in ministry.

42. I help people understand themselves, their relationships, and God better through artistic expression.

43. I can see through phoniness or deceit before it is evident to others.

44. I give hope to others by directing them to the promises of God.

45. I am effective at adapting the gospel message so that it connects with an individual's felt need.

46. I believe that God will help me to accomplish great things.

47. I manage my money well in order to free more of it for giving.

48. I willingly take on a variety of odd jobs around the church to meet the needs of others.

49. I genuinely believe the Lord directs strangers to me who need to get connected to others.

50. I am conscious of ministering to others as I pray.

51. I am committed, and schedule blocks of time for reading and studying scripture, to understand biblical truth fully and accurately.

52. I can adjust my leadership style to bring out the best in others.

53. I enjoy helping people sometimes regarded as underserving or beyond help.

54. I boldly expose cultural trends, teachings, or events which contradict biblical principles.

55. I like to provide guidance for the whole person — relationally, emotionally, spiritually, etc.

56. I pay close attention to the words, phrases, and meaning of those who teach.

SPIRITUAL GIFT ASSESSMENT

57. I can easily select the most effective course of action from among several alternatives.

58. I can identify and effectively use the resources needed to accomplish tasks.

59. I can adapt well to different cultures and surroundings.

60. I can visualize how something should be constructed before I build it.

61. I like finding new and fresh ways of communicating God's truth.

62. I tend to see rightness or wrongness in situations.

63. I reassure those who need to take courageous action in their faith, family, or life.

64. I invite unbelievers to accept Christ as their Savior.

65. I trust God in circumstances where success cannot be guaranteed by human effort alone.

66. I am challenged to limit my lifestyle in order to give away a higher percentage of my income.

67. I see spiritual significance in doing practical tasks.

68. I like to create a place where people do not feel that they are alone.

69. I pray with confidence because I know that God works in response to prayer.

70. I have insight or just know something to be true.

71. I set goals and manage people and resources effectively to accomplish them.

72. I have great compassion for hurting people.

73. I see most actions as right or wrong, and feel the need to correct the wrong.

74. I can faithfully provide long-term support and concern for others.

75. I like to take a systematic approach to my study of the Bible.

SPIRITUAL GIFT ASSESSMENT

76. I can anticipate the likely consequences of an individual's or a group's action.

77. I like to help organizations or groups become more efficient.

78. I can relate to others in culturally sensitive ways.

79. I honor God with my handcrafted gifts.

80. I apply various artistic expressions to communicate God's truth.

81. I receive affirmation from others concerning the reliability of my insights or perceptions.

82. I strengthen those who are wavering in their faith.

83. I openly tell people that I am a Christian and want them to ask me about my faith.

84. I am convinced of God's daily presence and action in my life.

85. I like knowing that my financial support makes a real difference in the lives and ministries of God's people.

86. I like to find small things that need to be done and often do them without being asked.

87. I enjoy entertaining people and opening my home to others.

88. When I hear about needy situations, I feel burdened to pray.

89. I have suddenly known some things about others, but did not know how I knew them.

90. I influence others to perform to the best of their capability.

91. I can look beyond a person's handicaps or problems to see a life that matters to God.

92. I like people who are honest and will speak the truth.

93. I enjoy giving guidance and practical support to a small group of people.

94. I can communicate scripture in ways that motivate others to study and want to learn more.

SPIRITUAL GIFT ASSESSMENT

95. I give practical advice to help others through complicated situations.

96. I enjoy learning about how organizations function.

97. I enjoy pioneering new undertakings.

98. I am good at and enjoy working with my hands.

99. I am creative and imaginative.

100. I can identify preaching, teaching, or communication which is not true to the Bible.

101. I like motivating others to take steps for spiritual growth.

102. I openly and confidently tell others what Christ has done for me.

103. I am regularly challenging others to trust God.

104. I give generously due to my commitment to stewardship.

105. I feel comfortable being a helper, assisting others to do their job more effectively.

106. I do whatever I can to make people feel that they belong.

107. I am honored when someone asks me to pray for them.

108. I discover important biblical truths when reading or studying scripture which benefit others in the body of Christ.

109. I am able to cast a vision that others want to be a part of.

110. I enjoy bringing hope and joy to people living in difficult circumstances.

111. I will speak God's truth, even in places where it is unpopular or difficult for others to accept.

112. I can gently restore wandering believers to faith and fellowship.

113. I can present information and skills to others at a level that makes it easy for them to grasp and apply to their lives.

114. I can apply scriptural truth that others regard as practical and helpful.

SPIRITUAL GIFT ASSESSMENT

115. I can visualize a coming event, anticipate potential problems, and develop backup plans.

116. I am able to orchestrate or oversee several church ministries.

117. I am able to design and construct things that help the church.

118. I regularly need to get alone to reflect and develop my imagination.

119. I can sense when demonic forces are at work in a person or situation.

120. I am able to challenge or rebuke others in order to foster spiritual growth.

121. I seek opportunities to talk about spiritual matters with unbelievers.

122. I can move forward in spite of opposition or lack of support when I sense God's blessing on an undertaking.

123. I believe I have been given an abundance of resources so that I may give more to the Lord's work.

124. I readily and happily use my natural or learned skills to help wherever needed.

125. I can make people feel at ease even in unfamiliar surroundings.

126. I often see specific results in direct response to my prayers.

127. I confidently share my knowledge and insights with others.

128. I figure out where we need to go and help others to get there.

129. I enjoy doing practical things for others who are in need.

130. I feel compelled to expose sin wherever I see it and to challenge people to repentance.

131. I enjoy patiently but firmly nurturing others in their development as believers.

132. I enjoy explaining things to people so that they can grow spiritually and personally.

133. I have insights into how to solve problems that others do not see.

OBSERVATION ASSESSMENT

Often, you will not be aware of what others have appreciated about you or noticed about your abilities in ministry situations. This indicator gives people who know you an opportunity to affirm your areas of possible spiritual giftedness.

DIRECTIONS

1. Your Participant's Guide contains three identical questionnaires. Remove all of them, give one questionnaire to each of three Christians who know you well, and ask them to complete and return it to you.

   Preferably, ask people who have observed you in a ministry context and understand Spiritual Gifts. If this is not possible, then ask people who know you well to make what observations they can from their general experience with you.

2. Since you will be giving your *Observation Assessment* to others to fill out and return to you, get started on these assignments as soon as possible. This way you won't run out of time, and you will be prepared for our next session.

3. When you receive the *Observation Assessment* back, compile the responses on the *Observation Assessment Summary* on pp.69-70 in your Participant's Guide.

OBSERVATION ASSESSMENT

I'd like your opinion!

I am seeking to better understand how God has equipped me for service in the church. One part of this process involves getting feedback from a few people who know me reasonably well. Your thoughts about the way I relate to others will be very helpful. Please take a few minutes to complete this sheet with your thoughtful consideration.

Opinions about: _LINDA_____

Provided by:_MoM_____

Relationship:_____

Please read each of the descriptions below. Mark each according to how well it describes the person this is for.

Y = Yes, very descriptive of this person
S = Somewhat or slightly descriptive
N = No, does not describe this person
? = Unsure, unknown, or not observed

In my opinion, this person has strengths in . . .

A. Developing strategies or plans to reach identified goals; organizing people, tasks, and events; helping organizations or groups become more efficient; creating order out of organizational chaos.

(Y) S   N   ?

B. Pioneering new undertakings (such as a new church or ministry); serving in another country or community; adapting to different cultures and surroundings; being culturally aware and sensitive.

Y   S   N (?)

C. Working creatively with wood, cloth, metal, paints, glass, etc.; working with different kinds of tools; making things with practical uses; designing or building things; working with his or her hands.

Y (S) N   ?

OBSERVATION ASSESSMENT

D. Communicating with variety and creativity; developing and using particular artistic skills (art, drama, music, photography, etc.); finding new and fresh ways to communicate ideas to others.

(Y) S N ?

E. Distinguishing between truth and error, good and evil; accurately judging character; seeing through phoniness or deceit; helping others to see rightness or wrongness in life situations.

(Y) S N ?

F. Strengthening and reassuring troubled people; encouraging or challenging people; motivating others to grow; supporting people who need to take action.

(Y) S N ?

G. Looking for opportunities to build relationships with nonbelievers; communicating openly and effectively about his or her faith; talking about spiritual matters with nonbelievers.

(Y) S N ?

H. Trusting God to answer prayer and encouraging others to do so; having confidence in God's continuing presence and ability to help, even in difficult times; moving forward in spite of opposition.

(Y) S N ?

I. Giving liberally and joyfully to people in financial need or projects requiring support; managing their money well in order to free more of it for giving.

(Y) S N ?

J. Working behind the scenes to support the work of others; finding small things that need to be done and doing them without being asked; helping wherever needed, even with routine or mundane tasks.

(Y) S N ?

K. Meeting new people and helping them to feel welcome; entertaining guests; opening his or her home to others who need a safe, supportive environment; setting people at ease in unfamiliar surroundings.

Y (S) N ?

OBSERVATION ASSESSMENT

L. Continually offering to pray for others; expressing
amazing trust in God's ability to provide;
evidencing confidence in the Lord's protection;
spending a lot of time praying.

 Y S N ?

M. Carefully studying and researching subjects he or
she wants to understand better; sharing his or her
knowledge and insights with others when asked;
sometimes gaining information that is not attained
by natural observation or means.

 Y S N ?

N. Taking responsibility for directing groups;
motivating and guiding others to reach important
goals; managing people and resources well;
influencing others to perform to the best of their
abilities.

 Y S N ?

O. Empathizing with hurting people; patiently and
compassionately supporting people through painful
experiences; helping those generally regarded as
undeserving or beyond help.

 Y S N ?

P. Speaking with conviction in order to bring change in
the lives of others; exposing cultural trends,
teachings, or events that are morally wrong or
harmful; boldly speaking truth even in places where
it may be unpopular.

 Y S N ?

Q. Faithfully providing long-term support and nurture
for a group of people; providing guidance for the
whole person; patiently but firmly nurturing others
in their development as believers.

 Y S N ?

R. Studying, understanding, and communicating
biblical truth; developing appropriate teaching
material and presenting it effectively;
communicating in ways that motivate others to
change.

 Y S N ?

OBSERVATION ASSESSMENT

S. Seeing simple, practical solutions in the midst of conflict or confusion; giving helpful advice to others facing complicated life situations; helping people take practical action to solve real problems.

Y S N ?

HERE ARE A FEW ADDITIONAL QUESTIONS:

Your responses will give me more specific feedback about your observations. Simply leave a question blank if you feel uncertain about how to answer.

1. What kinds of work do you think I am especially well suited to do in or through the church?	*Administration Deacon Give certain programs*
2. If you are familiar with the concept of spiritual gifts, which have you seen exhibited in my life? What have you specifically observed?	*Love, faithfulness Spirituality, giving Knowledge*
3. Are there any other observations or insights you have that would help me better understand my unique place of service in or through the church?	

Thank you for taking the time to complete this sheet. Your opinions are valuable to me in this process and I deeply appreciate your help.

OBSERVATION ASSESSMENT SUMMARY

Use this sheet to compile the *Observation Assessment* responses you received.

Whenever an observer marked "Y" for a Spiritual Gift, put *TWO* check marks in the appropriate block for that Spiritual Gift. Whenever an observer marked "S" for a Spiritual Gift, put *ONE* check mark in the appropriate block for that Spiritual Gift. Leave the blocks blank for "N" and "?" responses.

When you have done this for each *Observation Assessment*, total the number of check marks for each Spiritual Gift in the column headed "Row Total."

SPIRITUAL GIFT	OBSERVER 1	OBSERVER 2	OBSERVER 3	ROW TOTAL	
	MOM	*NANCY*	*KATHY J*		*MC*
A. Administration	2	2	1	5	1
B. Apostleship	0	1	0	1	
C. Craftsmanship	1	0	1	2	
D. Creative Communication	2	0	1	3	
E. Discernment	2	2	0	4	
F. Encouragement	2	2	1	5	
G. Evangelism	2	0	0	2	
H. Faith	2	2	1	5	2
I. Giving	2	0	0	2	

OBSERVATION ASSESSMENT SUMMARY

J . Helps	2	0	1	3
K . Hospitality	1	1	0	2
L . Intercession	2	2	0	4
M. Knowledge	2	2	2	6
N . Leadership	1	2	2	5
O . Mercy	2	1	1	4
P . Prophecy	1	0	0	1
Q . Shepherding	2	0	1½	3½
R . Teaching	2	0	2	4	3
S . Wisdom	2	1	2	5	3
T . Healing*				
U . Interpretation*				
V . Miracles*				
W. Tongues*				
Other Spiritual Gifts*				

* Although these gifts do not appear on the numbered list of descriptions given to your observers, they may be specifically mentioned by some of them in one of the open-ended questions. "Other" gifts include: Counseling, Celibacy, Martyrdom, Serving, etc.

When you have finished compiling the individual *Observation Assessments,* check what seem to you to be the Spiritual Gifts these persons have identified in you. Write these Spiritual Gifts on the lines in the *Observation Assessment* box on the next page.

OBSERVATION ASSESSMENT

I'd like your opinion!

I am seeking to better understand how God has equipped me for service in the church. One part of this process involves getting feedback from a few people who know me reasonably well. Your thoughts about the way I relate to others will be very helpful. Please take a few minutes to complete this sheet with your thoughtful consideration.

Opinions about: _____

Provided by: _Kathy Johnson_

Relationship: _friend_

Please read each of the descriptions below. Mark each according to how well it describes the person this is for.

    Y = Yes, very descriptive of this person
    S = Somewhat or slightly descriptive
    N = No, does not describe this person
    ? = Unsure, unknown, or not observed

In my opinion, this person has strengths in . . .
(circle your last response)

A. Developing strategies or plans to reach identified   Y **(S)** N ?
    goals; organizing people, tasks, and events; helping
    organizations or groups become more efficient;
    creating order out of organizational chaos.

B. Pioneering new undertakings (such as a new church   Y S **(N)** ?
    or ministry); serving in another country or
    community; adapting to different cultures and
    surroundings; being culturally aware and sensitive.

C. Working creatively with wood, cloth, metal, paints,   Y **(S)** N ?
    glass, etc.; working with different kinds of tools;
    making things with practical uses; designing or
    building things; working with his or her hands.

OBSERVATION ASSESSMENT

D. Communicating with variety and creativity; developing and using particular artistic skills (art, drama, music, photography, etc.); finding new and fresh ways to communicate ideas to others.

Y (S) N ?

E. Distinguishing between truth and error, good and evil; accurately judging character; seeing through phoniness or deceit; helping others to see rightness or wrongness in life situations.

Y S (N) ?

F. Strengthening and reassuring troubled people; encouraging or challenging people; motivating others to grow; supporting people who need to take action.

Y (S) N ?

G. Looking for opportunities to build relationships with nonbelievers; communicating openly and effectively about his or her faith; talking about spiritual matters with nonbelievers.

Y S (N) ?

H. Trusting God to answer prayer and encouraging others to do so; having confidence in God's continuing presence and ability to help, even in difficult times; moving forward in spite of opposition.

Y (S) N ?

I. Giving liberally and joyfully to people in financial need or projects requiring support; managing their money well in order to free more of it for giving.

Y S (N) ?

J. Working behind the scenes to support the work of others; finding small things that need to be done and doing them without being asked; helping wherever needed, even with routine or mundane tasks.

Y (S) N ?

K. Meeting new people and helping them to feel welcome; entertaining guests; opening his or her home to others who need a safe, supportive environment; setting people at ease in unfamiliar surroundings.

Y S (N) ?

OBSERVATION ASSESSMENT

S. Seeing simple, practical solutions in the midst of
conflict or confusion; giving helpful advice to
others facing complicated life situations; helping
people take practical action to solve real problems.

(Y) S N ?

HERE ARE A FEW ADDITIONAL QUESTIONS:

Your responses will give me more specific feedback about your
observations. Simply leave a question blank if you feel uncertain
about how to answer.

1. What kinds of work do you think I am especially well suited to do in or through the church?	*Shepherding Teaching*
2. If you are familiar with the concept of spiritual gifts, which have you seen exhibited in my life? What have you specifically observed?	*Shepherding Craftsmanship*
3. Are there any other observations or insights you have that would help me better understand my unique place of service in or through the church?	

*Thank you for taking the time to complete this sheet. Your opinions
are valuable to me in this process and I deeply appreciate your help.*

OBSERVATION ASSESSMENT

L. Continually offering to pray for others; expressing   **Y S N (?)**
    amazing trust in God's ability to provide;
    evidencing confidence in the Lord's protection;
    spending a lot of time praying.

M. Carefully studying and researching subjects he or   **(Y) S N ?**
    she wants to understand better; sharing his or her
    knowledge and insights with others when asked;
    sometimes gaining information that is not attained
    by natural observation or means.

N. Taking responsibility for directing groups;   **(Y) S N ?**
    motivating and guiding others to reach important
    goals; managing people and resources well;
    influencing others to perform to the best of their
    abilities.

O. Empathizing with hurting people; patiently and   **Y (S) N ?**
    compassionately supporting people through painful
    experiences; helping those generally regarded as
    undeserving or beyond help.

P. Speaking with conviction in order to bring change in   **Y S (N)?**
    the lives of others; exposing cultural trends,
    teachings, or events that are morally wrong or
    harmful; boldly speaking truth even in places where
    it may be unpopular.

Q. Faithfully providing long-term support and nurture   **(Y)(S) N ?**
    for a group of people; providing guidance for the
    whole person; patiently but firmly nurturing others
    in their development as believers.

R. Studying, understanding, and communicating   **(Y) S N ?**
    biblical truth; developing appropriate teaching
    material and presenting it effectively;
    communicating in ways that motivate others to
    change.

OBSERVATION ASSESSMENT

I'd like your opinion!

I am seeking to better understand how God has equipped me for service in the church. One part of this process involves getting feedback from a few people who know me reasonably well. Your thoughts about the way I relate to others will be very helpful. Please take a few minutes to complete this sheet with your thoughtful consideration.

Opinions about: _Linda McCown_

Provided by: _Nancy Hatfield_

Relationship: _friend (for approx. 15 years)_

Please read each of the descriptions below. Mark each according to how well it describes the person this is for.

Y = Yes, very descriptive of this person
S = Somewhat or slightly descriptive
N = No, does not describe this person
? = Unsure, unknown, or not observed

In my opinion, this person has strengths in . . .
(circle your last response)

A. Developing strategies or plans to reach identified goals; organizing people, tasks, and events; helping organizations or groups become more efficient; creating order out of organizational chaos.
GOOD AT MEETINGS
(Y) S N ?

B. Pioneering new undertakings (such as a new church or ministry); serving in another country or community; adapting to different cultures and surroundings; being culturally aware and sensitive.
Y (S) N ?

C. Working creatively with wood, cloth, metal, paints, glass, etc.; working with different kinds of tools; making things with practical uses; designing or building things; working with his or her hands.
Y S (N) ?

65

OBSERVATION ASSESSMENT

D. Communicating with variety and creativity; developing and using particular artistic skills (art, drama, music, photography, etc.); finding new and fresh ways to communicate ideas to others.   Y S Ⓝ ?

E. Distinguishing between truth and error, good and evil; accurately judging character; seeing through phoniness or deceit; helping others to see rightness or wrongness in life situations.   Ⓨ S N ?

F. Strengthening and reassuring troubled people; encouraging or challenging people; motivating others to grow; supporting people who need to take action.   Ⓨ S N ?

G. Looking for opportunities to build relationships with nonbelievers; communicating openly and effectively about his or her faith; talking about spiritual matters with nonbelievers.   Y S NⓀ?

H. Trusting God to answer prayer and encouraging others to do so; having confidence in God's continuing presence and ability to help, even in difficult times; moving forward in spite of opposition.   Ⓨ S N ?

I. Giving liberally and joyfully to people in financial need or projects requiring support; managing their money well in order to free more of it for giving.   Y S NⓀ?

J. Working behind the scenes to support the work of others; finding small things that need to be done and doing them without being asked; helping wherever needed, even with routine or mundane tasks.   Y S NⓀ?

K. Meeting new people and helping them to feel welcome; entertaining guests; opening his or her home to others who need a safe, supportive environment; setting people at ease in unfamiliar surroundings.   Y Ⓢ N ?

OBSERVATION ASSESSMENT

L. Continually offering to pray for others; expressing
amazing trust in God's ability to provide;
evidencing confidence in the Lord's protection;
spending a lot of time praying.

(Y) S N ?

M. Carefully studying and researching subjects he or
she wants to understand better; sharing his or her
knowledge and insights with others when asked;
sometimes gaining information that is not attained
by natural observation or means.

(Y) S N ?

N. Taking responsibility for directing groups;
motivating and guiding others to reach important
goals; managing people and resources well;
influencing others to perform to the best of their
abilities.

(Y) S N ?

O. Empathizing with hurting people; patiently and
compassionately supporting people through painful
experiences; helping those generally regarded as
undeserving or beyond help.

Y **(S)** N ?

P. Speaking with conviction in order to bring change in
the lives of others; exposing cultural trends,
teachings, or events that are morally wrong or
harmful; boldly speaking truth even in places where
it may be unpopular.

Y S N **(?)**

Q. Faithfully providing long-term support and nurture
for a group of people; providing guidance for the
whole person; patiently but firmly nurturing others
in their development as believers.

Y S N **(?)**

R. Studying, understanding, and communicating
biblical truth; developing appropriate teaching
material and presenting it effectively;
communicating in ways that motivate others to
change.

Y S N **(?)**

OBSERVATION ASSESSMENT

S. Seeing simple, practical solutions in the midst of   Y (S) N ?
conflict or confusion; giving helpful advice to
others facing complicated life situations; helping
people take practical action to solve real problems.

HERE ARE A FEW ADDITIONAL QUESTIONS:

Your responses will give me more specific feedback about your
observations. Simply leave a question blank if you feel uncertain
about how to answer.

1. What kinds of work do you think I am especially well suited to do in or through the church?	
2. If you are familiar with the concept of spiritual gifts, which have you seen exhibited in my life? What have you specifically observed?	
3. Are there any other observations or insights you have that would help me better understand my unique place of service in or through the church?	

*Thank you for taking the time to complete this sheet. Your opinions
are valuable to me in this process and I deeply appreciate your help.*

SPIRITUAL GIFTS SUMMARY

Use this page to compile the results of your *Observation Assessment* and the *Spiritual Gift Assessment*. This will complete this step in identifying your Spiritual Gift(s).

OBSERVATION ASSESSMENT	SPIRITUAL GIFT ASSESSMENT
(from pp.69-70 in this guide)	(from p.48 in this guide)
What Spiritual Gifts were observed by those who know you well?	What Spiritual Gifts did you identify on your *Spiritual Gift Assessment?*
	Admin
	Faith

Now, merge the results of the *Observation Assessment* and *Spiritual Gift Assessment* into a list of what you think are your Spiritual Gifts.

My Spiritual Gifts

_____

_____

_____

Transfer these Spiritual Gifts to p.124 in this guide.

SESSION 4 SUMMARY

Spiritual Gifts are mentioned in scripture.

Spiritual Gifts can be seen in action.

Spiritual Gifts are ultimately affirmed by the body of Christ.

What Can I Do To Make A Difference?

KEY SCRIPTURE PASSAGE: EPHESIANS 4:11–16

OVERVIEW

In this session you will:

1. Further clarify your Spiritual Gifts

2. List three general cautions when using your Spiritual Gifts

3. Link your primary Passion and primary Spiritual Gift

SPIRITUAL GIFT REFERENCE ASSESSMENT

The following reference material provides some additional information on each Spiritual Gift. Individuals with a particular Spiritual Gift typically evidence certain traits, some of which are listed. You may find these helpful in better understanding or confirming your Spiritual Gift(s).

DIRECTIONS

1. Locate in the *Spiritual Gift Reference Assessment* what you've identified as your primary Spiritual Gift.

2. As you read through the information about your Spiritual Gift, check any item you feel applies to you. If you begin to sense that the items are not particularly descriptive of you, take a look at what you've identified as your second Spiritual Gift. See if that may be a better match.

The *Spiritual Gift Reference Assessment* is provided to help you achieve a better under standing of your Spiritual Gift. Keep in mind that final affirmation of your Spiritual Gift comes from the body of Christ.

ADMINISTRATION

Literal Meaning: To pilot or steer a ship

Description: The gift of Administration is the divine enablement to understand what makes an organization function, and the special ability to plan and execute procedures that accomplish the goals of the ministry.

Distinctives: People with this gift
- ❏ Develop strategies or plans to reach identified goals
- ❏ Assist ministries to become more effective and efficient
- ❏ Create order out of organizational chaos
- ☑ Manage or coordinate a variety of responsibilities to accomplish a task
- ❏ Organize people, tasks, or events

Traits:
- ☑ Thorough
- ☑ Objective
- ☑ Responsible
- ☑ Organized
- ☑ Goal-oriented
- ☑ Efficient
- ☑ Conscientious

Cautions: People with this gift
- ❏ Need to be open to adjusting their plans, so that they don't stifle a leader's vision
- ❏ Could use people simply to accomplish goals without being concerned for their growth in the process
- ❏ Could fail to see God's purposes being fulfilled in the process of meeting a goal

References: 1 Cor. 12:28, Acts 6:1–7, Ex. 18:13–26

APOSTLESHIP

Literal Meaning: To be sent with a message

Description: The gift of Apostleship is the divine ability to start and oversee the development of new churches or ministry structures.

NOTE: While the "office" of apostle that the original disciples of Christ held is unique and no longer exists, the "role" of apostle continues today and functions through the Spiritual Gift of Apostleship.

Distinctives: People with this gift
- ❏ Pioneer and establish new ministries or churches
- ❏ Adapt to different surroundings by being culturally sensitive and aware
- ❏ Desire to minister to unreached people in other communities or countries
- ❏ Have responsibilities to oversee ministries or groups of churches
- ❏ Demonstrate authority and vision for the mission of the church

Traits:
- ❏ Adventurous
- ❏ Entrepreneurial
- ❏ Persevering
- ❏ Adaptable
- ❏ Culturally sensitive
- ❏ Risk-taking
- ❏ Cause-driven

Cautions: People with this gift
- ❏ Should be aware that misusing their authority can quench the Spirit in others
- ❏ Need to be affirmed and sent by the church
- ❏ Can be demanding and pessimistic

References: 1 Cor. 12:28–29, Eph. 4:11–12, Rom. 1:5, Acts 13:2–3

CRAFTSMANSHIP

Literal Meaning: To craft, design, build

Description: The gift of Craftsmanship is the divine enablement to creatively design and/or construct items to be used for ministry.

Distinctives: People with this gift
- ❏ Work with wood, cloth, paints, metal, glass and other raw materials
- ❏ Make things which increase the effectiveness of others' ministries
- ❏ Enjoy serving with their hands to meet tangible needs
- ❏ Design and build tangible items and resources for ministry use
- ❏ Work with different kinds of tools and are skilled with their hands

Traits:
- ❏ Creative
- ❏ Designer
- ❏ Handy
- ❏ Resourceful
- ❏ Practical
- ❏ Behind-the-scenes
- ❏ Helpful

Cautions: People with this gift
- ❏ Could fail to see that their gift is significant and one that make a spiritual contribution to the body
- ❏ Could use people to get things done instead of helping them grow in the process
- ❏ Should remember that the things they produce are just a means to the end and not the end itself

References: Ex. 31:3, 35:31–35, Acts 9:36–39, 2 Kings 22:5–6

CREATIVE COMMUNICATION

Literal Meaning: To communicate artistically

Description: The gift of Creative Communication is the divine enablement to communicate God's truth through a variety of art forms.

Distinctives: People with this gift
- ❏ Use the arts to communicate God's truth
- ❏ Develop and use artistic skills such as drama, writing, art, music, etc.
- ❏ Use variety and creativity to captivate people and cause them to consider Christ's message
- ❏ Challenge people's perspective of God through various forms of the arts
- ❏ Demonstrate fresh ways to express the Lord's ministry and message

Traits:
- ❏ Expressive
- ❏ Imaginative
- ❏ Idea-oriented
- ❏ Artistic
- ❏ Creative
- ❏ Unconventional
- ❏ Sensitive

Cautions: People with this gift
- ❏ Need to remember that art is not for art's sake, but it's to glorify God and edify others
- ❏ Could find evaluation and constructive criticism difficult to accept
- ❏ Might be uncooperative (because of ego, pride, or individualism) and need to work at being a team player

References: Ps. 150:3–5, 2 Sam. 6:14–15, Mark 4:2, 33

DISCERNMENT

Literal Meaning: To separate or make a distinction, differentiate

Description: The gift of Discernment is the divine enablement to distinguish between truth and error. It is able to discern the spirits, differentiating between good and evil, right and wrong.

Distinctives: People with this gift
- ❏ Distinguish truth from error, right from wrong, pure motives from impure
- ❏ Identify deception in others with accuracy and appropriateness
- ❏ Determine whether a word attributed to God is authentic
- ❏ Recognize inconsistencies in a teaching, prophetic message or interpretation
- ❏ Are able to sense the presence of evil

Traits:
- ❏ Perceptive
- ❏ Insightful
- ❏ Sensitive
- ❏ Intuitive
- ❏ Decisive
- ❏ Challenging
- ❏ Truthful

Cautions: People with this gift
- ❏ May struggle with how to express their perceptions, feelings or insights
- ❏ Could be harsh when confronting others, instead of speaking the truth in love
- ❏ Need to confirm their perceptions before speaking

References: 1 Cor. 12:10, Acts 5:1–4, Matt. 16:21–23

ENCOURAGEMENT

Literal Meaning: To come along side of

Description: The gift of Encouragement is the divine enablement to present truth so as to strengthen, comfort, or urge to action those who are discouraged or wavering in their faith.

Distinctives: People with this gift
❏ Come to the side of those who are discouraged to strengthen and reassure them
❏ Challenge, comfort, or confront others to trust and hope in the promises of God
❏ Urge others to action by applying biblical truth
❏ Motivate others to grow
❏ Emphasize God's promises and to have confidence in his will

Traits:
❏ Positive
❏ Motivating
❏ Challenging
❏ Affirming
❏ Reassuring
☑ Supportive
☑ Trustworthy

Cautions: People with this gift
❏ Can sometimes be overly optimistic, too simplistic or flattering
❏ Should first take time to understand where others are and what they really need
❏ May want to just say "positive" things to others and avoid being confrontational when it's needed

References: Rom. 12:8, Acts 11:22–24, Acts 15:30-32

EVANGELISM

Literal Meaning: To bring good news

Description: The gift of Evangelism is the divine enablement to effectively communicate the gospel to unbelievers so they respond in faith and move toward discipleship.

Distinctives: People with this gift
- ❑ Communicate the message of Christ with clarity and conviction
- ❑ Seek out opportunities to talk to unbelievers about spiritual matters
- ❑ Challenge unbelievers to faith and to become fully devoted followers of Christ
- ❑ Adapt their presentation of the gospel to connect with the individual's needs
- ❑ Seek opportunities to build relationships with unbelievers

Traits:
- ❑ Sincere
- ❑ Candid
- ❑ Respected
- ❑ Influential
- ❑ Spiritual
- ❑ Confident
- ❑ Commitment-oriented

Cautions: People with this gift
- ❑ Need to remember the Holy Spirit, not guilt, is the motivator in a person's decision for Christ
- ❑ Should avoid becoming critical of others by remembering that we are all "witnesses," but we are not all "evangelists"
- ❑ Need to listen carefully, because the same approach is not appropriate for everyone

References: Eph. 4:11, Acts 8:26–40, Luke 19:1–10

FAITH

Literal Meaning: To trust, have confidence, believe

Description: The gift of Faith is the divine enablement to act on God's promises with confidence and unwavering belief in God's ability to fulfill his purposes.

Distinctives: People with this gift
- ☑ Believe the promises of God and inspire others to do the same
- ❏ Act in complete confidence of God's ability to overcome obstacles
- ☑ Demonstrate an attitude of trust in God's will and his promises
- ❏ Advance the cause of Christ because they go forward when others will not
- ❏ Ask God for what is needed and trust him for his provision

Traits:
- ❏ Prayerful
- ❏ Optimistic
- ☑ Trusting
- ❏ Assured
- ❏ Positive
- ❏ Inspiring
- ☑ Hopeful

Cautions: People with this gift
- ❏ Need to act on their faith
- ❏ Should remember that those who speak with reason and desire to plan do not necessarily lack faith
- ❏ Should listen to and consider the counsel of wise and spirit-filled believers

References: 1 Cor. 12:9, 13:2, Heb. 11:1, Rom. 4:18–21

GIVING

Literal Meaning: To give part of, share

Description: The gift of Giving is the divine enablement to contribute money and resources to the work of the Lord with cheerfulness and liberality. People with this gift do not ask "How much money do I need to give to God?" but, "How much money do I need to live on?"

Distinctives: People with this gift
- ❏ Manage their finances and limit their lifestyle in order to give as much of their resources as possible
- ❏ Support the work of ministry with sacrificial gifts to advance the Kingdom
- ❏ Meet tangible needs that enable spiritual growth to occur
- ❏ Provide resources, generously and cheerfully, trusting God for his provision
- ❏ May have a special ability to make money so that they may use it to further God's work

Traits:
- ❏ Stewardship-oriented
- ❏ Responsible
- ❏ Resourceful
- ❏ Charitable
- ❏ Trusts in God
- ❏ Disciplined

Cautions: People with this gift
- ❏ Need to esteem their gift, remembering that giving money and resources is a spiritual contribution to the body of Christ
- ❏ Need to remember the church's agenda is determined by leaders, not by the giver's gift
- ❏ Need to guard against greed

References: Rom. 12:8, 2 Cor. 6:8, Luke 21:1-4

HEALING

Literal Meaning: To restore instantaneously

NOTE: The word is actually plural, "healings," which indicate that different kinds of healings are possible with this gift (i.e., emotional, relational, spiritual, physical, etc.).

Description: The gift of Healing is the divine enablement to be God's means for restoring people to wholeness.

Distinctives: People with this gift
❑ Demonstrate the power of God
❑ Bring restoration to the sick and diseased
❑ Authenticate a message from God through healing
❑ Use it as an opportunity to communicate a biblical truth and to see God glorified
❑ Pray, touch, or speak words that miraculously bring healing to one's body

Traits:
❑ Compassionate
❑ Trusts in God
❑ Prayerful
❑ Full of faith
❑ Humble
❑ Responsive
❑ Obedient

Cautions: People with this gift
❑ Need to remember that it is not always their faith or the faith of the sick that determines a healing, but God who determines it
❑ Need to realize that God does not promise to heal everyone who asks or is prayed for
❑ Should remember that Jesus did not heal everyone who was sick or suffering while he was on the earth

References: 1 Cor.12:9, 28, 30, Acts 3:1–16, Mark 2:1–12

HELPS

Literal Meaning: To take the place of someone

Description: The gift of Helps is the divine enablement to accomplish practical and necessary tasks which free-up, support, and meet the needs of others.

Distinctives: People with this gift
- Serve behind the scenes wherever needed to support the gifts and ministries of others
- See the tangible and practical things to be done and enjoy doing them
- Sense God's purpose and pleasure in meeting everyday responsibilities
- Attach spiritual value to practical service
- Enjoy knowing that they are freeing up others to do what God has called them to do

Traits:
- Available
- Willing
- Helpful
- Reliable
- Loyal
- Dependable
- Whatever-it-takes attitude

Cautions: People with this gift
- Need to esteem their gift, remembering that doing practical deeds is a *spiritual* contribution to the body of Christ
- Find it difficult to say "no"
- Need to be responsive to the priorities of leadership instead of setting their own agendas

References: 1 Cor. 12:28, Rom.12:7, Acts 6:1–4, Rom. 16:1–2

HOSPITALITY

Literal Meaning: To love strangers

Description: The gift of Hospitality is the divine enablement to care for people by providing fellowship, food, and shelter.

Distinctives: People with this gift
- ❏ Provide an environment where people feel valued and cared for
- ❏ Meet new people and help them to feel welcomed
- ❏ Create a safe and comfortable setting where relationships can develop
- ❏ Seek ways to connect people together into meaningful relationships
- ❏ Set people at ease in unfamiliar surroundings

Traits:
- ❏ Friendly
- ❏ Gracious
- ❏ Inviting
- ❏ Trusting
- ❏ Caring
- ❏ Responsive
- ❏ Warm

Cautions: People with this gift
- ❏ Should avoid viewing their gift as just "entertaining"
- ❏ Need to remember to ask *God* who he wants them to befriend and serve
- ❏ Should be careful not to cause stress in their own family when inviting others into their home

References: 1 Peter 4:9–10, Rom.12:13, Heb. 13:1–2

INTERCESSION

Literal Meaning: To plead on behalf of someone, intercede

Description: The gift of Intercession is the divine enablement to consistently pray on behalf of and for others, seeing frequent and specific results.

Distinctives: People with this gift
- ❏ Feel compelled to earnestly pray on behalf of someone or some cause
- ❏ Have a daily awareness of the spiritual battles being waged and pray
- ❏ Are convinced God moves in direct response to prayer
- ❏ Pray in response to the leading of the spirit, whether they understand it or not
- ❏ Exercise authority and power for the protection of others and the equipping of them to serve

Traits:
- ❏ Advocate
- ❏ Caring
- ☑ Sincere
- ☑ Peacemaker
- ☑ Trustworthy
- ❏ Burden-bearer
- ❏ Spiritually sensitive

Cautions: People with this gift
- ❏ Should avoid feeling that their gift is not valued, by remembering that interceding for others is their ministry and spiritual contribution to the body of Christ
- ❏ Should avoid using prayer as an escape an escape from fulfilling responsibilities
- ❏ Need to avoid a "holier than thou" attitude sometimes caused by extended times of prayer and spiritual intimacy with God

References: Rom. 8:26–27, John 17:9–26, 1 Tim. 2:1–2, Col. 1:9–12, 4:12–13

INTERPRETATION

Literal Meaning: To translate, interpret

Description: The gift of Interpretation is the divine enablement to make known to the body of Christ the message of one who is speaking in tongues.

Distinctives: People with this gift
- ❏ Respond to a message spoken in tongues by giving an interpretation
- ❏ Glorify God and demonstrate his power through this miraculous manifestation
- ❏ Edify the body by interpreting a timely message from God
- ❏ Understand an unlearned language and communicate that message to the body of Christ
- ❏ Are sometimes prophetic when exercising an interpretation of tongues for the church

Traits:
- ❏ Obedient
- ❏ Responsive
- ❏ Devoted
- ❏ Responsible
- ❏ Spiritually sensitive
- ❏ Discerning
- ❏ Wise

Cautions: People with this gift
- ❏ Need to remember that the message being interpreted should reflect the will of God and not man
- ❏ Should remember that this gift is to provide edification, it's to build up the church
- ❏ Use it in conjunction with tongues and it should be used in an orderly manner

References: 1 Cor. 12:10, 14:5, 14:26–28

KNOWLEDGE

Literal Meaning: To know

Description: The gift of Knowledge is the divine enablement to bring truth to the body through a revelation or biblical insight.

Distinctives: People with this gift
- ❏ Receive truth which enables them to better serve the body
- ❏ Search the scriptures for insight, understanding, and truth
- ❏ Have an unusual insight or understanding that serves the church
- ☑ Organize information for teaching and practical use
- ❏ Gain knowledge which was not attained by natural observation or means

Traits:
- ❏ Inquisitive
- ❏ Responsive
- ❏ Observant
- ❏ Insightful
- ❏ Reflective
- ☑ Studious
- ☑ Truthful

Cautions: People with this gift
- ❏ Need to be careful of this gift leading to pride ("knowledge puffs up")
- ❏ Should remember that it's God message, not theirs, when they give a word of knowledge to the church
- ❏ Need to remember with the increasing of knowledge comes the increasing of pain

References: 1 Cor. 12:8, Mark 2:6–8, John 1:45–50

LEADERSHIP

Literal Meaning: To stand before

Description: The gift of Leadership is the divine enablement to cast vision, motivate, and direct people to harmoniously accomplish the purposes of God.

Distinctives: People with this gift
- ❏ Provide direction for God's people or ministry
- ❏ Motivate others to perform to the best of their abilities
- ☑ Present the "big picture" for others to see
- ❏ Model the values of the ministry
- ❏ Take responsibility and establish goals

Traits:
- ❏ Influential
- ☑ Diligent
- ❏ Visionary
- ☑ Trustworthy
- ❏ Persuasive
- ❏ Motivating
- ❏ Goal-setter

Cautions: People with this gift
- ❏ Should realize their relational credibility takes time and is critical for leadership effectiveness
- ❏ Should remember that servant leadership is the biblical model, the greatest being the servant of all
- ❏ Do not need to be in a leadership "position" to use this gift

References: Rom. 12:8, Heb. 13:17, Luke 22:25–26

MERCY

Literal Meaning: To have compassion

Description: The gift of Mercy is the divine enablement to cheerfully and practically help those who are suffering or are in need, compassion moved to action.

Distinctives: People with this gift
- ❏ Focus upon alleviating the sources of pain or discomfort in suffering people
- ❏ Address the needs of the lonely and forgotten
- ❏ Express love, grace, and dignity to those facing hardships and crisis
- ❏ Serve in difficult or unsightly circumstances and do so cheerfully
- ❏ Concern themselves with individual or social issues that oppress people

Traits:
- ❏ Empathetic
- ❏ Caring
- ❏ Responsive
- ❏ Kind
- ❏ Compassionate
- ❏ Sensitive
- ❏ Burden-bearing

Cautions: People with this gift
- ❏ Need to be aware that rescuing people from their pain may be hindering God's work in them
- ❏ Need to guard against feeling "unappreciated," since some of the people helped will not show or express any appreciation
- ❏ Should guard against becoming defensive and angry about the sources of others' pain

References: Rom. 12:8, Matt. 5:7, Mark 10:46–52, Luke 10:25–37

MIRACLES

Literal Meaning: To do powerful deeds

Description: The gift of Miracles is the divine enablement to authenticate the ministry and message of God through super-natural interventions which glorify him.

Distinctives: People with this gift
- ❏ Speak God's truth and have it authenticated by an accompanying miracle
- ❏ Express confidence in God's faithfulness and ability to manifest his presence
- ❏ Bring the ministry and message of Jesus Christ with power
- ❏ Claim God to be the source of the miracle and Glorify him
- ❏ Represent Christ and through the gift point people to a relationship with Christ

Traits:
- ❏ Bold
- ❏ Venturesome
- ❏ Authoritative
- ❏ God-fearing
- ❏ Convincing
- ❏ Prayerful
- ❏ Responsive

Cautions: People with this gift
- ❏ Need to remember that miracles are not necessarily caused by faith
- ❏ Should avoid viewing this gift as a personal responsi-bility, remembering that God determines the location and timing of his deeds
- ❏ Need to guard against the temptation to call on the Lord's presence and power for selfish purposes

References: 1 Cor. 12:10, 28–29, John 2:1–11, Luke 5:1–11

PROPHECY

Literal Meaning: To speak before

Description: The gift of Prophecy is the divine enablement to reveal truth and proclaim it in a timely and relevant manner for understanding, correction, repentance, or edification. There may be immediate or future implications.

Distinctives: People with this gift
- ❏ Expose sin or deception in others for the purpose of reconciliation
- ❏ Speak a timely word from God causing conviction, repentance, and edification
- ❏ See truth that others often fail to see and challenge them to respond
- ❏ Warn of God's immediate or future judgment if there is no repentance
- ❏ Understand God's heart and mind through experiences he takes them through

Traits:
- ❏ Discerning
- ❏ Compelling
- ❏ Uncompromising
- ❏ Outspoken
- ❏ Authoritative
- ❏ Convicting
- ❏ Confronting

Cautions: People with this gift
- ❏ Need to be aware that listeners may reject the message if not spoken with love and compassion
- ❏ Need to avoid pride which can create a demanding or discouraging Spirit that hinders the gift
- ❏ Should remember that discernment and scripture must support and agree with each prophecy

References: Rom.12:6, 1 Cor. 12:10, 28, 13:2, 2 Peter 1:19–21

SHEPHERDING

Literal Meaning: To shepherd a flock

Description: The gift of Shepherding is the divine enablement to nurture, care for, and guide people toward on-going spiritual maturity and becoming like Christ.

Distinctives: People with this gift
- ❏ Take responsibility to nurture the whole person in their walk with God
- ❏ Provide guidance and oversight to a group of God's people
- ❏ Model with their life what it means to be a fully devoted follower of Jesus
- ❏ Establish trust and confidence through long-term relationships
- ❏ Lead and protect those within their span of care

Traits:
- ❏ Influencing
- ❏ Nurturing
- ❏ Guiding
- ❏ Discipling
- ❏ Protective
- ❏ Supportive
- ❏ Relational

Cautions: People with this gift
- ❏ Should remember that God judges those who neglect or abuse their oversight responsibilities
- ❏ Need to be aware that the desire to feed and support others can make it difficult to say "no"
- ❏ Should realize that some of those being nurtured will grow beyond the shepherd's own ability and need to be freed to do so

References: Eph. 4:11–12, 1 Peter 5:1–4, John 10:1–18

TEACHING

Literal Meaning: To instruct

Description: The gift of Teaching is the divine enablement to understand, clearly explain, and apply the word of God, causing greater Christ-likeness in the lives of listeners

Distinctives: People with this gift
- ❏ Communicate biblical truth that inspires greater obedience to the word
- ☑ Challenge listeners simply and practically with the truths of scripture
- ☑ Present the whole counsel of God for maximum life change
- ☑ Give attention to detail and accuracy
- ❏ Prepare through extended times of study and reflection

Traits:
- ❏ Disciplined
- ❏ Perceptive
- ☑ Teachable
- ☑ Authoritative
- ❏ Practical
- ☑ Analytical
- ☑ Articulate

Cautions: People with this gift
- ❏ Should avoid pride that may result from their "superior" biblical knowledge and understanding
- ❏ Could become too detailed when teaching and fail to make life application
- ❏ Should remember that their spirituality is not measured by how much they know

References: Rom.12:7, 1 Cor. 12:28–29, Acts 18:24–28, 2 Tim. 2:2

TONGUES

Literal Meaning: Tongue, language

Description: The gift of Tongues is the divine enablement to speak, worship, or pray in a language unknown to the speaker. People with the gift may receive a spontaneous message from God which is made known to his body through the gift of Interpretation.

Distinctives: People with this gift
- Express with an interpretation a word by the Spirit which edifies the body
- Communicate a message given by God for the church
- Speak in a language they have never learned and do not understand
- Worship the Lord with unknown words too deep for the mind to comprehend
- Experience an intimacy with God which inspires them to serve and edify others

Traits:
- Sensitive
- Prayerful
- Responsive
- Trusting
- Devoted
- Spontaneous
- Receptive

Cautions: People with this gift
- Should remain silent in the church if there is no interpreter
- hould avoid expecting others to manifest this gift which may cause in authen ticity of the Spirit
- Should remember that all the gifts, including this one, are to edify others

References: 1 Cor. 12:10, 28–30, 13:1, 14:1–33, Acts 2:1–11

WISDOM

Literal Meaning: To apply truth practically

Description: The gift of Wisdom is the divine enablement to apply spiritual truth effectively to meet a need in a specific situation.

Distinctives: People with this gift
- ☑ Focus on the unseen consequences in determining the next steps to take
- ❑ Receive an understanding of what is necessary to meet the needs of the body
- ❑ Provide divinely given solutions in the midst of conflict and confusion
- ❑ Hear the Spirit provide direction for God's best in a given situation
- ☑ Apply spiritual truth in specific and practical ways

Traits:
- ☑ Sensible
- ❑ Insightful
- ☑ Practical
- ☑ Wise
- ☑ Fair
- ❑ Experienced
- ☑ Common Sense

Cautions: People with this gift
- ❑ Could fail to share the wisdom that God has given them
- ❑ Need to avoid having others develop a dependence upon them, which may weaken their faith in God
- ❑ Need to be patient with others who do not have this gift

References: 1 Cor. 12:8, James 3:13–18, 1 Cor. 2:3–14, Jer. 9:23–24

HUDDLE GROUP: OTHER'S SPIRITUAL GIFTS

DIRECTIONS

1. Further clarify your Spiritual Gift(s) by sharing with your group:

   a. Your primary Spiritual Gift and why you think you have it

   b. Cautions you think you have to be aware of when using this Spiritual Gift

2. Listen to the others in your group as they share their Spiritual Gifts to get a better understanding of other Spiritual Gifts.

GENERAL CAUTIONS

- _Projection_

"Do as I do."

- _Elevation_

"I have a more important Spiritual Gift than you do."

- _Rejection_

"I don't have a Spiritual Gift."

LINKING SPIRITUAL GIFTS TO PASSION

Situation 1: Same Passion, Different Gifts

People serving in different positions within the same ministry:

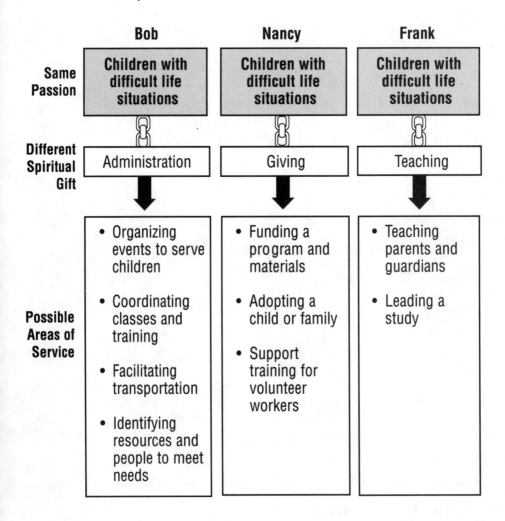

	Bob	**Nancy**	**Frank**
Same Passion	Children with difficult life situations	Children with difficult life situations	Children with difficult life situations
Different Spiritual Gift	Administration	Giving	Teaching
Possible Areas of Service	• Organizing events to serve children • Coordinating classes and training • Facilitating transportation • Identifying resources and people to meet needs	• Funding a program and materials • Adopting a child or family • Support training for volunteer workers	• Teaching parents and guardians • Leading a study

LINKING SPIRITUAL GIFTS TO PASSION

Situation 2: Different Passions, Same Gift

People serving in different ministries in similar positions:

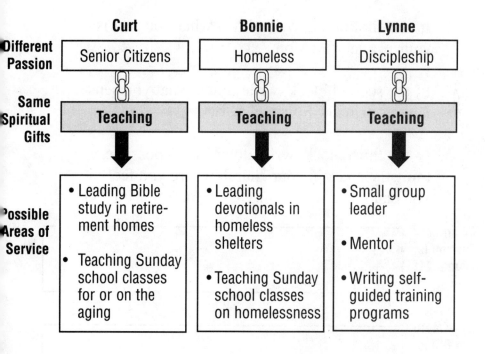

	Curt	**Bonnie**	**Lynne**
Different Passion	Senior Citizens	Homeless	Discipleship
Same Spiritual Gifts	Teaching	Teaching	Teaching
Possible Areas of Service	• Leading Bible study in retirement homes • Teaching Sunday school classes for or on the aging	• Leading devotionals in homeless shelters • Teaching Sunday school classes on homelessness	• Small group leader • Mentor • Writing self-guided training programs

LINKING SPIRITUAL GIFTS TO PASSION

INDIVIDUAL ACTIVITY: LINKING SPIRITUAL GIFTS TO PASSION

Directions

1. In the first block, write down what you feel is your primary Passion.

2. In the second block, write down what you sense is your primary Spiritual Gift.

3. In the third block, write down some possible ministry areas in your church where you feel you can serve with your Passion and Spiritual Gift.

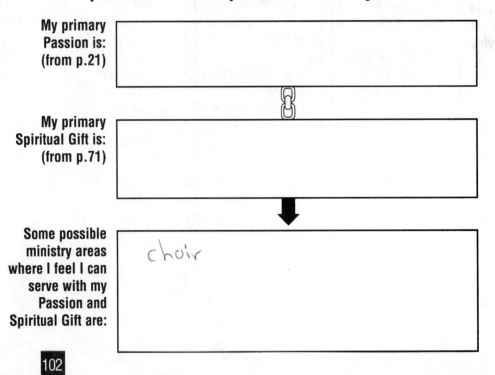

My primary
Passion is:
(from p.21)

My primary
Spiritual Gift is:
(from p.71)

Some possible
ministry areas
where I feel I can
serve with my
Passion and
Spiritual Gift are:

choir

SESSION 5 SUMMARY

We explored Spiritual Gifts by using the *Spiritual Gift Reference Assessment*.

We learned three general cautions when using Spiritual Gifts

- Projection

- Elevation

- Rejection

We linked our primary Passion and Spiritual Gift.

What's Love Got To Do With It?

KEY SCRIPTURE PASSAGE: 1 CORINTHIANS 13:1–8

O V E R V I E W

In this session you will:

1. List the results of serving with love and without love

2. Identify the differences between Servility and Servanthood

3. Apply the principles of Servanthood to an actual ministry situation

4. Identify one aspect of Servanthood you will concentrate on and a practical step you can take toward it

LOVE AND SERVING

And now I will show you the most excellent way.
(1 Cor. 12:31b)

*If I speak in the tongues of men and of angels, but
have not love, I am only a resounding gong or a
clanging cymbal. If I have the gift of prophecy
and can fathom all mysteries and all knowledge,
and if I have a faith that can move mountains, but
have not love, I am nothing. If I give all I possess
to the poor and surrender my body to the flames,
but have not love, I gain nothing.* (1 Cor. 13: 1–3)

Spiritual Gifts expressed without love do not reflect
who God is and do not have a _____

_____ .

*Love is patient, love is kind. It does not envy, it
does not boast, it is not proud. It is not rude, it is
not self-seeking, it is not easily angered, it keeps
no record of wrongs. Love does not delight in
evil but rejoices with the truth. It always protects,
always trusts, always hopes, always perseveres.
Love never fails.* (1 Cor. 13:4–8a)

SERVILITY AND SERVANTHOOD

Servility: serving without love

Servanthood: serving with love

WHAT IS OUR MOTIVATION FOR SERVING?

	SERVILITY	SERVANTHOOD
SERVES OUT OF:	• _____ It's an "I-have-to" kind of attitude.	• _____ It is an "I want to serve God!" attitude.
IS MOTIVATED TO SERVE BY A CONCERN FOR:	• _____ In Servility the motivation is driven by "what will others say if I don't serve, or if I don't serve in this ministry, or don't serve in this way, or don't commit this kind of time?"	• _____ In Servanthood we serve because we have fellowship and communion with God. We understand that ultimately we have an audience of One.
SERVES WITH THE ATTITUDE OF:	• _____ Servility aims to do the minimum necessary to get by and fulfill the basics.	• _____ Servanthood is willing to go outside the "job description."
HAS A MINISTRY MINDSET THAT SAYS:	• _____ Servility wants to advance its own agenda, and is asking "What's in it for me?"	• _____ Servants look up and say, "Lord, what would YOU have me do at this time? God, how could my life best honor YOU? How can I make a difference today in the way you have enabled me to touch lives?"

WHAT IS OUR MOTIVATION FOR SERVING?

SERVES WITH A SPIRIT OF:	• _____ When we serve out of Servility, we look at what we did and say "Hey, **I** did that, **I** have something to offer, aren't **I** something." **I** … **I** … **I** … **I**.	• _____ Servanthood says "GOD did that! GOD has given me a Spiritual Gift and has filled me with his Spirit to empower me for the faithful and meaningful expression of that Spiritual Gift. GOD has used me to have an impact in a person's life."
THE RESULTS ARE:	• _____ Believers prompted by Servility try to build up and draw attention to themselves.	• _____ Servanthood says "Don't look at me, I am glad to serve you; give God the glory, isn't he wonderful?"

In the same way, let your light shine before men, that they may see your good deeds and praise your Father in heaven. (Matt. 5:16)

By this all men will know that you are my disciples, if you love one another. (John 13:35)

HUDDLE GROUP: SERVANTHOOD

DIRECTIONS

1. Each person discuss one aspect of Servanthood (serving with love) that you would like to concentrate on.

2. Identify one practical step you can take toward it.

One aspect of Servanthood that you would like to concentrate on as you serve:

One practical step you can take toward it:

SESSION 6 SUMMARY

Results of serving without love is that there is no kingdom impact.

Differences were identified between Servility and Servanthood.

Principles of Servanthood were applied to an actual ministry situation.

How Can I Do It With Style?

KEY SCRIPTURE PASSAGE: PSALM 139:13–16

OVERVIEW

In this session you will:

1. Identify the three key characteristics of Personal Style

2. Identify the two key elements of Personal Style

3. Determine your Personal Style using the *Personal Style Assessment*

4. Compile your *Servant Profile*

5. Identify two ministry possibilities that reflect your *Servant Profile*

PERSONAL STYLE CHARACTERISTICS

1. Personal Style is God-given.

2. There is no right or wrong Personal Style.

3. Personal Style answers the

   "   " question.
   _____How_____

For you created my inmost being; you knit me together in my mother's womb. I praise you because I am fearfully and wonderfully made; your works are wonderful, I know that full well. My frame was not hidden from you when I was made in the secret place. When I was woven together in the depths of the earth, your eyes saw my unformed body. All the days ordained for me were written in your book before one of them came to be. (Ps. 139:13–16)

Write your name

A. _____

B. _____

PERSONAL STYLE ELEMENTS

TASK-ORIENTED ⟷ PEOPLE-ORIENTED

This scale describes how we receive and focus our emotional energy.

Task-
Oriented
Energized
by doing
things

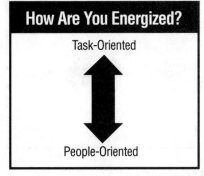

How Are You Energized?

Task-Oriented

People-Oriented

People-
Oriented
Energized by
interacting
with *people*

If you are Task-Oriented:

The primary content of your ministry should be accomplishing _____ that serve people.

Your primary focus should be on _____ .

If you are People-Oriented:

The primary content of your ministry should be more involved with _____

_____ .

Your primary focus should be on _____

_____ .

Both People-Oriented and Task-Oriented value developing relationships and meeting goals, but each has a primary and secondary means of achieving them.

PERSONAL STYLE ELEMENTS

UNSTRUCTURED ⬌ STRUCTURED

This scale describes how you prefer to organize your-self.

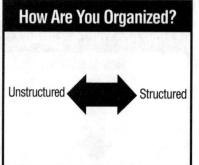

Unstructured
Prefer to have lots of options and *flexibility*

Structured
Prefer to plan and bring *order* to their lives

If you are Unstructured:

Your ministry position should be

_____ .

Your relationships with others should be

_____ .

If you are Structured:

Your ministry position should be

_____ .

Your relationships with others should be

_____ .

Both Unstructured and Structured value being organized, but each has a different approach to organization.

PERSONAL STYLE ASSESSMENT

DIRECTIONS

1. For each item, check the word you think best describes what you would prefer to do or be in most situations.

2. Do not answer according to what you feel is expected by a spouse, family member, employer, etc.

3. Select the behavior or perspective that would come naturally to you if you knew there were no restrictions on or consequences for your personal expression.

HOW ARE YOU ORGANIZED?

1. While on vacation I prefer to	be spontaneous	1 2 3 ④ 5	follow a set plan
2. I prefer to set guidelines that are	general	1 ②3 4 5	specific
3. I prefer to	leave my options open	1 2 ③ 4 5	settle things now
4. I prefer projects that have	variety	1 2 ③ 4 5	routine
5. I like to	play it by ear	1 2 3 ④ 5	stick to a plan
6. I find routine	boring	1 2 3 ④ 5	restful
7. I accomplish tasks best	by working it out as I go	1 2 3 ④ 5	by following a plan

How are you organized? **0= 25** **Total**

PERSONAL STYLE ASSESSMENT

HOW ARE YOU ENERGIZED?

1. I'm more comfortable	doing things for people	1 (2) 3 4 5	being with people
2. When doing a task, I tend to	focus on the goal	(1) 2 3 4 5	focus on relationships
3. I get more excited about	advancing a cause	1 (2) 3 4 5	creating community
4. I feel I have accomplished something when I've	gotten a job done	1 (2) 3 4 5	built a relationship
5. It is more important to start a meeting	on time	1 (2) 3 4 5	when everyone gets there
6. I'm more concerned with	meeting a deadline	1 (2) 3 4 5	maintaining the team
7. I place a higher value on	action	1 2 3 (4) 5	communication

How are you energized? **E=** 15 **Total**

TABULATE YOUR PROFILE

1. On the grid on the next page, put an X on the "O" scale that corresponds to your "O" total from page 117.

2. On the grid on the next page, put an X on the "E" scale that corresponds to your "E" total from above.

3. Draw a vertical line through the X marked on the "O" scale.

PERSONAL STYLE ASSESSMENT

TABULATE YOUR PROFILE, CONT.

4. Draw a horizontal line through the number circled on the "E" scale.

5. Your Personal Style is indicated where the lines meet (see sample).

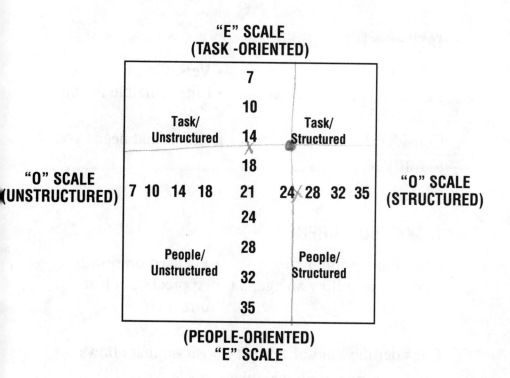

Sample

Personal Style is indicated where the lines meet

"E" SCALE
(TASK -ORIENTED)

	7	
	10	
Task/ Unstructured	14	Task/ Structured
	18	
"O" SCALE (UNSTRUCTURED) 7 10 14 18	21	24 28 32 35 "O" SCALE (STRUCTURED)
	24	
People/ Unstructured	28	People/ Structured
	32	
	35	

(PEOPLE-ORIENTED)
"E" SCALE

"E" SCALE
(TASK -ORIENTED)

7

10

Task/
Unstructured   14   Task/
Structured

18

"O" SCALE
(UNSTRUCTURED)   7 10 14 18   21   24 28 32 35   "O" SCALE
(STRUCTURED)

24

People/
Unstructured   28   People/
Structured

32

35

(PEOPLE-ORIENTED)
"E" SCALE

TRANSFER YOUR PERSONAL STYLE TO PAGE 124.
IN THIS GUIDE.

THE FOUR PERSONAL STYLE QUADRANTS

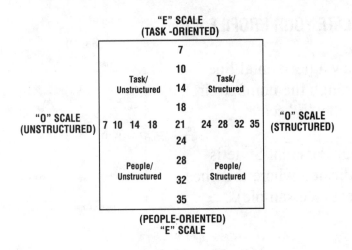

"E" SCALE
(TASK -ORIENTED)

"O" SCALE
(UNSTRUCTURED)

"O" SCALE
(STRUCTURED)

(PEOPLE-ORIENTED)
"E" SCALE

TASK/UNSTRUCTURED

- General guidelines
- Helps wherever needed

- Versatile
- Likes tangible results

Consider the kind of ministry position that needs you to fulfill a _____ of responsibilities.

TASK/STRUCTURED

- Getting the job done
- Prefers to follow an agenda

- Focused on results
- Appreciates clear direction

Consider the kind of ministry position that allows you to know clearly what the _____ are and _____ the task is to be accomplished.

THE FOUR PERSONAL STYLE QUADRANTS

PEOPLE/UNSTRUCTURED

- Spontaneous situations
- Relates well to others
- Very conversational
- Tends to be flexible

Consider the kind of ministry position that gives you the freedom to respond to people _____.

PEOPLE/STRUCTURED

- Defined relationships
- Projects warmth
- Familiar surroundings
- Enjoys familiar relationships

Consider the kind of ministry position that will enable you to interact with people in more _____ or _____ .

PERSONAL STYLE INTENSITY

"E" SCALE
(TASK -ORIENTED)

Mike Sally **7**	
10	
Task/ **14**	Task/
Unstructured	Structured
Phil Nancy **18**	

"O" SCALE
(UNSTRUCTURED)   **7 10 14 18 21**   **24 28 32 35**   **"O" SCALE**
(STRUCTURED)

24	
28	
People/	People/
Unstructured **32**	Structured
35	

(PEOPLE-ORIENTED)
"E" SCALE

PERSONAL STYLE SUMMARY

Personal Style does _____our

behavior, but it doesn't _____it.

COMPILE YOUR SERVANT PROFILE

DIRECTIONS

1. Write your Personal Style in the blank provided.

2. If you haven't already written in your Passion and Spiritual Gift, please do that too.

PASSION
(FROM PAGE 21)

_____

SPIRITUAL GIFTS
(FROM PAGE 71)

1. _____

2. _____

3. _____

PERSONAL STYLE
(FROM PAGE 119)

_____

HUDDLE GROUP: LIST MINISTRY POSSIBILITIES

DIRECTIONS

1. Share your *Servant Profile* with your huddle group (as the other members of your huddle group share their *Servant Profiles*, note their names, Passions, Spiritual Gifts, and Personal Styles in the "Mini-*Servant Profiles*" boxes).

2. Have the group suggest some ministry possibilities, and write these possibilities in the space provided on the next page.

3. Check two of the ministry possibilities that interest you most.

Don't feel limited by the ministries your church may or may not have.

MINI-*SERVANT PROFILES*

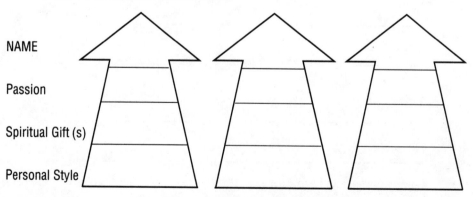

NAME

Passion

Spiritual Gift (s)

Personal Style

HUDDLE GROUP: LIST MINISTRY POSSIBILITIES

MINISTRY POSSIBILITIES AT MY CHURCH THAT INTEREST ME ARE:

❑ _____

_____

❑ _____

_____

❑ _____

_____

❑ _____

_____

❑ _____

_____

SESSION 7 SUMMARY

Personal Style answers the *how* question.

Personal Style elements
- Task-Oriented/People-Oriented, how we are *energized*
- Unstructured/Structured, how we are *organized*

Servant Profile
- God's design for *you*

Serving Is For A Lifetime!

KEY SCRIPTURE PASSAGE: 1 PETER 4:10

O V E R V I E W

In this session you will:

1. List two principles of serving for a lifetime

2. Identify the difference between Unique Contributions and Community Contributions

3. Identify two factors that affect your ability to make a Unique or Community contribution

4. Review the second step of Network's Process, Consultation

SERVICE IS FOR A LIFETIME

Therefore, I urge you, brothers, in view of God's mercy, to offer your bodies as living sacrifices, holy and pleasing to God—this is your spiritual act of worship. (Rom. 12:1)

Worship is expected *for a lifetime.*

As each one has received a special gift, employ it in serving one another, as good stewards of the manifold grace of God. (1 Peter 4:10 NASB)

Stewardship is required *for a lifetime.*

You, my brothers, were called to be free. But do not use your freedom to indulge the sinful nature; rather, serve one another in love. Gal. 5:13)

Service is *for a lifetime.*

UNIQUE AND COMMUNITY CONTRIBUTION

UNIQUE CONTRIBUTION

Your Unique Contribution is serving in a way that
expresses your _____
of Passion, Spiritual Gifts, and Personal Style.

COMMUNITY CONTRIBUTION

Community Contributions involve the _____
_____ of the
church to provide a place for worship and ministry.

UNIQUE AND COMMUNITY CONTRIBUTION

FACTORS THAT AFFECT YOUR ABILITY TO MAKE A UNIQUE OR COMMUNITY CONTRIBUTION

AVAILABILITY

SPIRITUAL MATURITY

THE CONSULTATION

Your consultant will work with you to identify areas of ministry for which your *Servant Profile* indicates a possible fit.

For your consultation, complete pages 140-48 in the appendix.

NETWORK SUMMARY

Why we are to serve:

- Glorify God
- Edify others

How we are to serve, *Servant Profile:*

- Passion, answers the *where* question
- Spiritual Gifts, answers the *what* question
- Personal Style, answers the *how* question

When we serve we are to serve:

- As a body
- In love

What's done in love will last forever.

Service is for a lifetime!

THE SPIRITUAL GIFTS

Administration

Apostleship

Craftsmanship

Creative Communication

Discernment

Encouragement

Evangelism

Faith

Giving

Healing

Helps

Hospitality

Intercession

Interpretation

Knowledge

Leadership

Mercy

Miracles

Prophecy

Shepherding

Teaching

Tongues

Wisdom

COURSE EVALUATION

Network Material

1. To what extent did this program meet your expectations in terms of value and quality?

5	4	3	2	1
Went Beyond Expectations		Met Expectations		Less Than Expected

2. How much learning did you experience during this program?

5	4	3	2	1
Significant		Moderate		Little

3. How relevant is what you learned to your church or ministry?

5	4	3	2	1
Highly Relevant		Somewhat Relevant		Not Relevant

4. Would you recommend that others attend this program?

5	4	3	2	1
Yes Definitely		Possibly		Definitely not

5. What aspects of this program were most useful?

_____

_____

6. What aspects of this program were least useful?

_____

_____

COURSE EVALUATION

7. What, if anything, should have been included that was not?

_____

_____

Instructor

8. To what extent did the instructor demonstrate depth of under-standing and credibility with regard to the material?

5	4	3	2	1
To a very great extent		To some extent		To little or no extent

9. To what extent did the instructor have a motivating effect, contributing to your learning?

5	4	3	2	1
To a very great extent		To some extent		To little or no extent

10. To what extent did the instructor's interaction with the participants facilitate your learning?

5	4	3	2	1
To a very great extent		To some extent		To little or no extent

11. Comments:

_____

_____

_____

_____

DON'T CONFUSE SPIRITUAL GIFTS WITH

TALENTS

Talents can be an indicator to your giftedness but do not necessarily equate to your Spiritual Gift.

We would make a distinction between Spiritual Gifts and natural talents. While Spiritual Gifts are unique to the believer, talents are common to all. Both are God-given. Just as your experiences and character traits may indicate a particular Spiritual Gift, so may your talents. The affirmation of any Spiritual Gift must be consistent with glorifying God and edifying others.

FRUIT OF THE SPIRIT

Fruit of the Spirit is the mark of spiritual maturity listed in Galatians 5:22–23: "love, joy, peace, patience, kindness, goodness, faithfulness, gentleness and self-control." It relates to the development of character. It is a "be" quality, while Spiritual Gifts are "do" qualities.

Both Fruit of the Spirit and Spiritual Gifts should be evident in the life of believers. Both are important for a well-rounded, God-honoring life.

SPIRITUAL DISCIPLINES

Spiritual Disciplines include personal Bible study, prayer, fasting, tithing, and other practices that help us grow in faith, control our sinful desires, and develop character. Spiritual Disciplines help us *grow* in our relationship to God.

TITLE / JOB

DON'T CONFUSE SPIRITUAL GIFTS WITH

Spiritual Gifts help us *serve* in the body of Christ. The relationship between Spiritual Gifts and Spiritual Disciplines is illustrated by the following comparison:

SPIRITUAL GIFTS	SPIRITUAL DISCIPLINES
• Evangelism	• Witnessing
• Intercession	• Prayer
• Knowledge	• Study

MINISTRY POSITIONS

At church, we refer to some people as "pastor," "teacher," or "leader." These titles may or may not match exactly with their Spiritual Gift. For example, though we have many small group leaders, they may not all have the gift of Leadership, nor do they need that gift to be a small group leader (position). Some may have the gift of Shepherding, some Encouragement, some Teaching, and some Leading. Not all Sunday School teachers (position) have the gift of Teaching. We call them "teachers," yet they may have other gifts. These titles are valuable to us for purposes of communication around church, yet we need to remember that these titles do not always match up exactly with the person's Spiritual Gifts.

PREPARING FOR YOUR CONSULTATION

HOW TO MAXIMIZE YOUR CONSULTATION

1. Before your consultation:

   - Pray for wisdom and discernment for you and the consultant.
   - Review your *Servant Profile*, and prepare to discuss your Passion, Spiritual Gifts, and Personal Style with your consultant.
   - Review the information on Availability and Spiritual Maturity on pages 141-43, and complete the *Personal Resources Survey* on pages 145-48.
   - Identify ministries that reflect your uniqueness and in which you are very interested.
   - Commit to working with the consultant to prioritize the ministry opportunities which seem to be the most natural expressions of who God made you to be.

2. If for any reason you are unable to keep a scheduled appointment with your consultant, please call that person 48 hours in advance. Your thoughtfulness is appreciated.

3. After the consultation, contact the specific ministries you identified for possible involvement within two weeks after your consultation, while ideas and descriptions are still fresh.

4. Devote time to prayer, reflection, and exploration concerning your involvement in a particular ministry.

5. If you have any additional questions, call your consultant. Your consultant is a volunteer whose ministry is to serve you.

PREPARING FOR YOUR CONSULTATION

AVAILABILITY

Our season or stage in life may affect our availability.

Do you have young children? Are you married? Single?
Single with children? What other issues influence the time
you have available for service?

How much do you travel during the week? How far do you
live from where your potential ministry   commitment would
be? What activities are you involved in during the week?

What is your level of availability? Do you feel as if you are
out of time? Are you spending time on other activities that
could take a lesser priority compared to making your unique
contribution (certain time wasters, for example). We support
a balanced life, but also realize that serving is a priority.

After assessing current time commitments and priorities, do
you have the time to begin making your unique contribution?
If not, that does not preclude you from serving. You could
find a related position that better fits your schedule at this
time in your life, while planning to make your unique contribution at some point in the future.

PREPARING FOR YOUR CONSULTATION

List your major time commitments:

_____

_____

_____

_____

_____

_____

_____

_____

Check the level of availability to which you are able to commit at this time:

❏ Limited: one to two hours per week
❏ Moderate: two to four hours per week
❏ Significant: four or more hours per week

If for some reason you are unavailable at this time, discuss with your consultant future ministry possibilities.

PREPARING FOR YOUR CONSULTATION

SPIRITUAL MATURITY

If you were to take a spiritual snapshot of your relationship with Christ, which of the following would best describe how you see yourself at this time?

☐ SEEKER?

You are gaining a better understanding of Christ and the Christian faith, but you have not yet personally trusted Jesus for the forgiveness of your sins. You are still investigating Christianity, still seeking truth.

☐ NEW/YOUNG BELIEVER?

You have recently become a Christian, and you are excited and enthused about your new walk with Jesus Christ, or you have been a Christian for some time, but you are just now learning what Jesus meant when He promised abundant life. In either case, you need to grow further in your understanding of the basics of the Christian faith and of what it means to walk daily in a personal relationship with Christ.

☐ STABLE/GROWING BELIEVER?

You are confident of God's faithfulness and his ability to accomplish his will in your life. You are teachable and sensitive to the Spirit's leading. You exhibit the stability that comes from knowing Christ, regularly worshipping with his people, and actively pursuing a life of greater devotion.

☐ LEADING/GUIDING BELIEVER?

You have reached a high level of maturity in the faith. You are able to model faithfulness and inspire other believers. You can lead by example and guide others in a deeper understanding of what it means to walk personally with Jesus Christ.

PREPARING FOR YOUR CONSULTATION

PERSONAL RESOURCES SURVEY — 1

PERSONAL

Name _____ Network Session Month /Year ____,____

Address _____ Apt# _____

City _____ State _____ Zip _____

Home Phone (____) _____ Work Phone (____)_____

Birth Date _____ ❏ Male ❏ Female

FAMILY

Marital Status: ❏ Single ❏ Married

Spouse's name: _____ Birthdate: _____

Children names: _____ ❏ M ❏ F Birthdate: _____

_____ ❏ M ❏ F Birthdate: _____

_____ ❏ M ❏ F Birthdate: _____

_____ ❏ M ❏ F Birthdate: _____

_____ ❏ M ❏ F Birthdate: _____

CHURCH

When did you start attending the church? Month/Year: _____

Are you a member? ❏ Yes ❏ No

Small Groups: ❏ I am in one (Leader's name _____)

❏ I would like to be in one

❏ I used to be in one (Leader's name _____)

❏ Other: _____

CURRENT MINISTRY INVOLVEMENT

Which ministries are you now involved in?   ❏ None

Ministry _____ Leader_____

List other ministries or community groups outside the church in which you are involved:

Ministry/Group_____

PAST MINISTRY INVOLVEMENT

Which ministries have you been involved in in the past? ❏ None

Ministry_____ Leader_____

List other ministries or community groups outside the church in which you have been involved:

Ministry/Group _____

Ministry/Group _____

PREPARING FOR YOUR CONSULTATION

PERSONAL RESOURCES SURVEY — 2

SERVANT PROFILE AND CONSULTATION SUMMARY

**Complete Prior To
Your Consultation**

I have a **Passion** for:

1. _____
2. _____

My **Spiritual Gifts** are:

1. _____
2. _____

**Shaded Area To Be Completed By
Consultant**

Passion

1. _____
2. _____

Spiritual Gifts

1. _____
2. _____
3. _____

My **Personal Style** is:
- ❑ People-Oriented/Structured
- ❑ Task-Oriented/Structured
- ❑ People-Oriented/Unstructured
- ❑ Task-Oriented/Unstructured

I would describe my **spiritual maturity** as:
- ❑ Seeker
- ❑ Stable/growing believer
- ❑ New/young believer
- ❑ Leading/guiding believer

I would describe my current **availability** as:
- ❑ Limited, 1-2 hrs
- ❑ Significant, 4+ hrs
- ❑ Moderate, 2-4 hrs
- ❑ Not sure

I would like to know more about the following ministries:

_____

_____

The following ministries were identified as possible places of service:

A. _____ B. _____ C. _____

Consultant: _____ Phone: _____

Comments: _____

_____

_____

PREPARING FOR YOUR CONSULTATION

PERSONAL RESOURCES SURVEY — 3

EMPLOYMENT

❏ I am employed   ❏ Self Employed   ❏ Unemployed

Name of Company _____

Title/Responsibilities _____

Product or service _____

EDUCATION

❏ High School   ❏ Some College   ❏ Other

❏ College   ❏ Masters Degree

❏ Doctorate   ❏ Professional Degree

SPIRITUAL JOURNEY

How did you come to know Christ personally? How do you maintain your relationship?

_____

_____

_____

_____

_____

_____

_____

_____

_____

_____

_____

_____

_____

_____

PREPARING FOR YOUR CONSULTATION

PERSONAL RESOURCES SURVEY — 4

In addition to your *Servant Profile*, please go through each area, carefully marking the boxes which indicate talents or skills in which you have proven ability. In other words, indicate areas in which you have demonstrated a reasonable amount of confidence and competence. You are not making a commitment to serve in any area where you check a box, but we would like to have this information on file in case of special needs. Be honest and fair in your self-evaluation.

PROFESSIONAL SERVICES
- ☐ Mental Health
- ☐ Social Work
- ☐ Financial
- ☐ Dental
- ☑ Medical
- ☐ Chiropractic
- ☐ Legal
- ☐ Accounting
- ☐ Bookkeeping
- ☐ Taxes
- ☐ Nursing
- ☐ Landscaping
- ☐ Carpet Cleaning
- ☐ Window Washing
- ☐ Engineer: _____
- ☐ Lifeguard
- ☐ Counseling
- ☐ Career Counseling
- ☐ Unemployment
- ☐ Day Care Director
- ☐ Law Enforcement
- ☐ Personnel Manager
- ☐ Public Relations
- ☐ Advertising
- ☐ Television: _____
- ☐ Radio
- ☐ Computer Prog.
- ☐ Paramedic/EMT
- ☐ Systems Analyst
- ☐ Journalist/Writer
- ☐

ART
- ☐ Layout
- ☑ Photography
- ☐ Graphics
- ☐ Multi-Media
- ☐ Typesetting
- ☐ Crafts
- ☐ Artist
- ☐ Banners
- ☐ Decorating

TEACHING OR ASSISTING
- ☐ Preschool
- ☐ Elementary
- ☐ Junior High
- ☐ Senior High
- ☐ Single Adults (18-29)
- ☑ Single Adults (30+)
- ☐ Couples
- ☐ Men's Group
- ☑ Women's Group
- ☐ Tutoring
- ☐ Learning Disabled
- ☐ Researcher
- ☐ Aerobics
- ☐ Budget Counselor
- ☐ _____

MECHANICAL
- ☐ Copier Repair
- ☐ Diesel Mechanic
- ☐ Auto Mechanic
- ☐ Small engine Repair
- ☐ Mower Repair
- ☐ Machinist
- ☐ _____

OFFICE SKILLS
- ☐ Typing (40+ wpm)
- ☑ Word Processing
- ☐ Receptionist
- ☐ Office Manager
- ☐ Data Entry
- ☐ Filing
- ☐ Mail Room
- ☐ Library
- ☐ Transcription
- ☐ Shorthand
- ☐

MISSIONS
- ☐ Missionary
- ☐ Evangelism
- ☐

THEATRICAL
- ☐ Actor/Actress
- ☐ Poet
- ☐ Dance
- ☐ Mime
- ☐ Puppets
- ☐ Clowning
- ☐ Audio Production
- ☐ Sound/Mixing
- ☐ Lighting
- ☐ Set Construction
- ☐ Set Design
- ☐ Stage Hand
- ☐ Script Writer
- ☐ _____

CONSTRUCTION
- ☐ General Contractor
- ☐ Architect
- ☐ Carpenter: General
- ☐ Carpenter: Finish
- ☐ Carpenter: Cabinet
- ☐ Electrician
- ☐ Plumbing
- ☐ Heating
- ☐ Air Conditioning
- ☐ Painting
- ☐ Papering
- ☐ Masonry
- ☐ Roofing
- ☐ Telephones
- ☐ Drywall Finishing
- ☐ Concrete
- ☐ Carpet Installer
- ☐ Interior Design
- ☐ Drafting
- ☐

WORKING WITH
- ☐ Handicapped
- ☐ Hearing Impaired (Signing)
- ☐ Incarcerated
- ☐ Learning Disabilities
- ☑ Nursing Homes/Shut-Ins
- ☑ Hospital Visitation
- ☐ Meals on Wheels
- ☐ Housing for Homeless
- ☐ _____

GENERAL HELP
- ☐ Cashier
- ☐ Child Care
- ☐ Customer Service
- ☐ Food Service
- ☐ Gardening
- ☐ Building Maintenance
- ☐ Grounds Maintenance
- ☐ Transportation
- ☐ Snow Removal
- ☐ Catering/Cooking
- ☐ Weddings
- ☐ Bookstore
- ☐ Tape Duplication
- ☐ Plant Care (Indoor)
- ☐ Sports Official
- ☐ Sports Instructor
- ☐ _____

MUSICAL
- ☐ Choir Director
- ☑ Choir
- ☐ Soloist
- ☑ Instrument
- ☐ Composer
- ☐ Arranger
- ☐ Piano Tuner
- ☐

Are there any other products, specific resources, skills, interests, talents, abilities, or unique opportunities (example: permitted access to specialized purchasing/discounts for the church) that you would like to offer to the church?

I understand that this information will be made available only to responsible and appropriate staff and ministry leaders at this church.

Signature: _____ Date: _____

THE NEXT STEP

NAME: _____

The next step for me is to contact the following ministries and complete the final step of Network: Service.

The consultant and I agree the ministry position to consider at this time would be:

> **M:**

Ministry A

Contact person _____

Phone_____

Ministry B

Contact person _____

Phone _____

Ministry C

Contact person _____

Phone_____

My Consultant was _____

Phone Date _____

BIBLIOGRAPHY

Background
The New Reformation, Greg Ogden, Zondervan
Pouring New Wine Into Old Wineskins, Aubrey Malphurs, Baker Books

General
Serving One Another, Gene Getz, Victor Books
The New Reformation, Greg Ogden, Zondervan
Unleashing the Church, Frank Tillapaugh, Regal Books
Unleashing Your Potential, Frank Tillapaugh, Regal Books
Partners In Ministry, James Garlow, Beacon Hill Press of Kansas City
The Body, Chuck Colson, Word Publishing
What Color Is Your Parachute?, Richard Bolles, Ten Speed Press
Improving Your Serve, Charles Swindoll, Word Publishing

Passion
The Truth About You, Arthur Miller/Ralph Mattson, Ten Speed Press

Spiritual Gifts
Spiritual Gifts, Bobby Clinton, Horizon House
Spiritual Gifts, David Hocking, Promise Publishing
Team Ministry, Larry Gilbert, Church Growth Institute
Spiritual Gifts Can Help Your Church Grow, Peter Wagner, Regal Books
Finding (and Using) Your Spiritual Gifts, Tim Blanchard, Tyndale House
Discovering Spiritual Gifts, Paul Ford, Fuller Institute

Personal Style
Please Understand Me, David Keirsey/Marily Bates,
   Prometheus Nemesis Book Co.
Understanding How Others Misunderstand You, Ken Vogues/Ron Braund,
   Moody
The Delicate Art of Dancing With Porcupines, Bob Phillips, Regal Books

Other Resources
Serving Sessions, Bill Hybels, Seeds Tapes
   (Willow Creek Community Church)

Network Ministry Support
Willow Creek Association
P. O. Box 3188
Barrington, IL   60011-3188
Phone: 708/765-0070
Fax: 708/765-5046

Network Ministries International
27355 Betanzos
Mission Viejo, CA 92692
Phone: 800-588-8833